Justice Now

Operating in God's Courts of Heaven

Annie Blouin

Life Press Publishing

© Copyright 2025 by Annie Blouin

Published by Life Press Publishing

Printed in the United States of America

ISBN 978-0-9978847-2-2

Religion/ Christian Life/ Spiritual Growth

Books by Annie Blouin are available at:

www.annieblouin.com
www.amazon.com

Acknowledgements

Thank you to Jesus, Father, and Holy Spirit. I love You and want to see You get all that You paid for. Thanks for partnering with me.

Joe, you mean the world to me. Thanks for doing life together. Thanks for serving, loving, and living. I love you.

My family. Madeleine & Nick, Hadassah and Auggie. Grace & Tate. Joey. You all are everything to me. Here's to the future together.

Beka, thanks for the encouragement that this book is worthy to read and should go to publication.

And to my lunch lady friends! You all encourage me so much. I could not have written this without all your prayers.

Margaret and Kim. Thanks for editing this book and getting it ready for the masses. I couldn't have done it without both of you. Thanks so much.

Contents

Courts Prayers

I.

Introduction to God's Courts of Heaven

The Courts of Heaven is a framework for believers to approach God with their concerns, recognizing His authority as judge, and utilizing the legal basis of the blood of Jesus to seek resolution and break free from spiritual opposition. The courts address spiritual strongholds. They identify and challenge demonic influence based on legal claims and they seek God's justice and resolution. They present cases to God and seek His judgment and intervention.

The Courts of Heaven are God's way of bringing justice to earth. Our earthly systems are legislated through heaven's courts. Just like our earthly court systems bring justice or legislate what goes on on earth, it is even more so how heaven's courts legislate our activities here. If we don't show up in heaven's courts, we can lose because the enemy is showing up to accuse us. However, if we do show up and take our authority, we can rule and reign the way we were designed. We were designed to bring heaven to earth.

The courts are the power in God's system for bringing justice on earth as it is in heaven. If you understand the power of the courts, you will use them. It is where the authority of the believer, the power of God, and the holiness of God make sense.

The Courts of Heaven are a powerful tool for us to bring heaven to earth. They are a way of bringing God's justice to earth for all areas in which we and He are involved. You will see you and your family receive breakthroughs in the areas where you have been given God's prophetic words and in areas you have need. And then as you become proficient in the courts, you will see the world win breakthroughs. The courts are a way for us to operate in and bring God's kingdom. The enemy is operating against us in the courts and if we don't show up with Jesus, the enemy is allowed to rule against us.

Prior to 2015 I hadn't really understood the courts. I had heard about the concept a decade before but thought it was prophetic, beautiful language and not really a place where justice could be accomplished. In 2007 I had even received a prophetic word about teaching people about the courts of heaven, but I thought the word was an abstraction of language rather than practical steps to teach.

My husband and I had a vision in 2015 about the courts of heaven. It was quite astonishing and will probably impact the rest of our lives. We had gotten a prophetic word from a friend who said God wanted to talk to both of us through our seer gift and we should lie down, hold hands, and see what God had to show us. We took that seriously and wanted to see what God had for us. I started because I'm not as visual as my husband is. We went back and forth sharing what we were seeing, and we realized we were seeing the same things.

In the vision, I told my husband I saw an angel sitting on steps. I saw that the steps were marble and there was a marble building behind them. Even though I saw the details of marble steps with the marble building, I only told Joe that an angel was sitting on steps. He told me that the steps were marble, and the marble building was at the top of the steps. At this time, we knew we were seeing the same thing, so we went confidently forward. What we saw next was that as we walked up the steps, the angel stood up and walked us into the building. The building was a court room. It was very regal looking, both inside and outside, even more so than our Supreme Court. Jesus was at the defense desk where the angel left us. Father God was the judge and was sitting at the bench. The enemy was about four feet tall, had a stack of documents about three feet tall in his hands, and he looked like a weasel. Court was in session. The enemy was railing against us with the documents as his evidence. The documents were all the generational sin against our family lines. As we watched, Father God banged down His gavel and said, "Enough! Time for restoration and restitution for the Blouins. First up is a new vehicle." And the vision ended.

At the end of the vision, Joe and I were very surprised. We knew something significant had happened but didn't know what to expect. At that point in our lives our finances were very low and because of the warfare we'd fought, it had been impossible to buy another vehicle. We were a family of five and had one vehicle. The kids were teenagers, and we had moved from Redding, California to Raleigh, North Carolina the year before.

Within a month, we bought another vehicle and within nine months, we bought two more vehicles. Within eighteen months of that vision, we were able to buy a house. It was a time of restoration and restitution!

In our previous lives in Redding, we followed God's leading and there was much poverty in our lives. In the beginning of the journey, God told me He was in it and not to run from it. At the end of the eight years, I had a dream where a pastor told me that in our Redding season we took down four generational giants against our family line. I saw that our radical obedience to Jesus had taken the giants down. However, in our new lives in North Carolina, poverty was not supposed to follow us there. It only did because we hadn't taken care of all the generational repentance yet. There can be a time in life when poverty occurs because of the leadings of Jesus but it should be just a season and not a lifetime. Jesus told us in John 10:10 that "the thief does not come except to steal, and to kill, and to destroy. I have come that they may have life, and that they may have it more abundantly." This life includes prosperity to have resources to preach the Gospel and to leave wealth to your children's children (Proverbs 13:22).

If you had asked me if we had done generational repentance at the time of the vision, I would have said yes. In fact, I would have thought we were basically done with the repentance because of all the prayers of repentance we had done over the course of many years. We were not new Christians at this time and had been saved almost twenty years on my end and twenty-five on my husband's. Yet, in the vision, there was a three-foot-tall stack of documents against us and our family line. What we learned from all of this was that any generational repentance that wasn't done, the enemy would use against us in court.

If you relate to this in your life, I encourage you to do the generational repentance that is mentioned in the appendix of this book. If it includes some things you've already done, great. If it doesn't, then you're covered. It's too important of a topic to overlook. Even if your stack of documents is only a foot high compared to our three-foot-tall stack, it still needs taking care of.

THE NEED FOR THE COURTS

I've learned that the Courts of Heaven is God's justice system. He set it up. This is how He operates. Earth looks like Heaven in that our court system, even when the system is corrupt, is supposed to bring justice. As believers, we're also supposed to operate in heaven's court system to bring justice to the earth. Prior to learning about heaven's courts, I know I would occasionally operate in them at God's discretion by praying a certain decree that would leave me feeling the issue was settled and I'd quickly see an answer to the prayer. I just didn't know that's where I was because I didn't see anything when I prayed. You may have already operated in the courts and not known it. For me, looking back, it was when a major victory would come. God would first have me forgive any offenders, repent on their behalf, and then make a declaration for the situation. As soon as I would do that, I would know those situations were finished. I wouldn't need to pray anymore. It may still take a few years for the outcome, but it was already wrapped up in heaven. The only reason I knew it was done was through the ways God spoke to me. Sometimes it'd be through Him saying it, other times it would just feel finished supernaturally. Anytime I "felt" the situation was finished, the outcome would happen even if it took a few years. Now that God has released the revelation of the courts of heaven to me, it is my responsibility to operate in them on a regular basis.

When we initially go into the courts of heaven, we are working to free ourselves from the generational sin that has enveloped our family lines. As we repent, we are at the defense attorney's desk with Jesus. We agree with the sin, repent from it, and God washes us white as snow. He talks about not remembering our sin any longer once it's confessed. Hebrews 10:17-18 tells us, 'Then He adds: "Their sins and lawless acts I will remember no more." And where these have been forgiven, sacrifice for sin is no longer necessary.' (NIV). However, after we have confessed all our generational sin, we then switch desks for all future work. We are then at the prosecutorial desk where, with Jesus, we determine what goes on for earth and the enemy no longer gets a say. It's an offensive approach and very powerful for what goes on here on earth.

I knew we'd gone on offense to legislate bringing heaven to earth but previously only thought about the courts as defense. We must get to this approach because it's powerful. My friend, CariAnn Watson, saw it in a vision. She had an encounter with God where He told her we switch to the prosecutorial side. We go on offense. Once sin is repented for and that court work is done, then we're no longer at the defensive end where the enemy has a say.

I was teaching a course in Raleigh on the prophetic, at the church's school of revival, from 2015-2019. One of my students was a woman named Pamela. I asked her to go for coffee because she's a rich treasure of experience and love for the Lord. At our coffee appointment I told her about the vision we'd had nine months before and how we'd bought the vehicles. I was talking about God's provision and how provided for we were. She said, "Yes that's the Courts of Heaven, and we take people through all the time." I thought it was a one-time thing because we'd had a vision. I was astounded and asked her to teach me. She also told me about how important generational repentance was before going into the Courts. She said if you don't do the generational repentance first, for defense, you will likely receive the breakthrough you're looking for, but the enemy will still go after you in many areas of your life. I knew this had to do with the 3-foot-tall stack of documents in the enemy's hand in our court case. Despite all the generational repentance we'd already done, there was a lot more to do.

Pamela was already working with Jacquelin and Dan Hanselman. Jacquelin and her husband, Dan, had written the book on ancient generational repentance—Silencing the Accuser: Restoration of Your Birthright—after a long desert season. The Lord had shown them how important it was to do. Through a few interactions with them, and through prayer, I witnessed to the truth of the book.

Generational repentance is praying aloud prayers that say, to God, that you're sorry for what you or your family line has done. There is a real contriteness to the prayers. When you understand what you and your family have done, sorrow comes with it. If you're a feeler, it will feel somber, heavy, and sorrowful. You may yawn or burp or cough during the prayers. That usually is a sign of deliverance. Deliverance occurs because of repentance. As you continue to pray, joy will start to come into the atmosphere. As the darkness leaves, heaven erupts with great joy.

After my coffee with Pamela, my husband and I then spent time repenting generationally. We repented aloud the prayers in Silencing the Accuser by Jacquelin Hanselman, a freemasonry repentance prayer found online on jubileeresources.org, and then we broke off the judgments of freemasonry in Overturning the False Verdicts of Freemasonry by Ron Horner. I have found these books to be very comprehensive. In my estimation, by observing our family and my students, I believe the books remove 98% of the generational sin. You can listen to the Lord as to whether any more sin needs to be confessed in your family line. We personally also had to do a Buddhist repentance prayer because that was in my husband's line as well as a few other prayers that the Lord directed us to.

We knew this would be important for our generations. As soon as I finished the freemasonry book, the Lord spoke to me and told me I was done with freemasonry repentance. Prior to Ron Horner's book coming out in 2018, the Lord would have me, every couple of years, do a freemasonry repentance prayer. I think it was because it was a way to keep freemasonry off my back before I could get rid of the judgments. Removing the judgments is an important part of the process.

We also did individual prayers on kanaanministries.org. There's a druid repentance prayer on there that removed some inaccuracies from my prophetic gift. My family came from Ireland and England where, four to five hundred years ago, druids were the false prophets of the day. They walked in the prophetic, but it was very tainted and full of the enemy. I recommend prophetic people do that prayer. You never know how your prophetic gift of today is impacted by the sin from ancient generations ago.

I ask everyone who wants to operate in the courts of heaven to do generational repentance first. Even if some of it is redundant, I guarantee there will be things you haven't yet done. The next section details the why behind the generational repentance so that we can operate first defensively and then offensively in the courts of heaven.

Ask God how free you are in your family line and how much generational repentance you need to still do. Journal His thoughts here.

Family Dynamics:
Acknowledgment of individual sins and how family patterns, such as abuse or addiction, perpetuate negative behaviors across generations.

_____
_____
_____
_____
_____
_____
_____

Mental Health and Emotional Well-being:
Inherited mental health issues or emotional trauma within families.

_____
_____
_____
_____
_____
_____
_____

Historical Healing:
Repentance for historical injustices that continue to affect generations.

_____
_____
_____
_____
_____
_____
_____

Other:

_____
_____
_____
_____
_____
_____

WHY THE COURTS

Why do we go into the Courts? Because the enemy is there, accusing you and your family whether you go in or not. Just like in the natural, if you don't go into court you lose. The rulings and judgments are against you if you don't show up. That's what we experienced before our vision. In our vision, the angel was sitting down waiting for us. How long had he been there? Had he been standing there before and eventually gotten tired from years or decades or generations of waiting?

Generational repentance removes the ability for the enemy to accuse you. Our defenses are, at that point, shored up. I took a woman from Michigan through the courts. She was interested in a business breakthrough for herself. She saw Deuteronomy 5:9-10 come to life.

"You shall not bow down to them nor serve them. For I, the Lord your God, am a jealous God, visiting the iniquity of the fathers upon the children to the third and fourth generations of those who hate Me, but showing mercy to thousands, to those who love Me and keep My commandments."

She saw a vision of herself standing on a big platform with a huge wall in front of her. It looked like the old train depots. On the wall were listed all her generational family sins. As she repented for them, they flipped to nothing. As she finished, the wall was blank; the demons were left with nothing to see or have to use against her or her family. This was the system by which the demonic would always grab hold of a sin, use it as justification, and go harass the family. As she repented, there was nothing further to grab onto and the angels took the demons out of the room. She understood that her defenses were now fortified, and she could do offensive work without any demonic harassment for the past.

Please understand the distinction between her own sins and her generational sins. When she got saved, Jesus forgave her. He says that her sins are as forgotten as the east is from the west—Jeremiah 31:34 "I will forgive their wickedness and will remember their sins no more." So, her sins were forgiven and forgotten. That is the case for every person who has ever gotten saved and reconciled to God. It does not cover those in the family line who did not reconcile themselves to God and those family sins are still active for the demons to grab hold of and harass family members.

This is huge. Please understand this point. We all know people who have stood up for God and had all hell break loose against them. It's because the demons look at their generational wall and access unconfessed generational sin to legally harass them. When the wall is wiped clean through repentance, most of the demonic activity against them is prohibited. Offensive measures may then go through with much greater speed and major progress.

The courts then become an offensive tool. We go into court to judge spirits—the enemy—and to get justice both for things out of order and for building things going forward. Psalms 92:13 describes it very well, "Those who are planted in the house of the Lord shall flourish in the courts of our God."

The courts of heaven have quick fruit! How fast the answers come is why I keep going back into the courts. It is my primary tool. Examples of fruit I have experienced personally are tumors disappearing, money increasing, jobs returning, relationships restored, marriages taking place and healing in marital relationships, babies being conceived and born, and prodigals returning home. These are all at the personal level as I work with people. Many breakthroughs have also come for the nation based on metron* cases in the corporate realm.

If you're called to the family mountain of influence**, you've likely had all kinds of horrible things happen to your family. It's to keep you from walking in your area of influence and to make your heart sad. What you'll find is, the courts of heaven stop the enemy from harassing your family line, and the work you do will be prosperous for the family mountain of influence.

We know of a family called to the mountain of family. They had done the personal generational repentance and done the personal court work yet hadn't done the offensive side of the court work. They've had many things go wrong in their extended family through the years. As soon as they moved forward with the offensive court work, they took one of their son's destinies

*Metron can be defined as a sphere of influence. 2 Corinthians 10:13-14 says God has assigned us a sphere within which we are to operate.
**The 7 mountains of influence shape the culture of every nation. They are media, government, education, family, religion, arts and entertainment, and business.

through the courts and his entire life changed in a week's time. He got into medical school, sold a car, and much money came in for his future. It was radical how fast everything changed for the better. Would it have changed without the courts? It probably would have changed because they're a praying family, but it may have taken more time.

It was time for the prophetic words of God to happen and partnering with God in His courts brought a swift result. Psalm 84:10 sums it up very well, "For a day in Your courts is better than a thousand elsewhere, I would rather be a doorkeeper in the house of my God than dwell in the tents of the wicked." NIV

The billion-soul harvest that Bob Jones prophesied about many years ago has begun. We have a lot of people coming into the kingdom that don't want to go decades without getting all their effects taken care of. We can help them with this.

The repentance and courts process gets rid of the enemy and speeds up the process. However, there is still a sanctification process of growth in God that won't be short circuited. The growth takes time and the courts won't eliminate that, but the enemy part will be gone, "Therefore, my beloved, as you have always obeyed, not as in my presence only, but now much more in my absence, work out your own salvation with fear and trembling; for it is God who works in you both to will and to do for His good pleasure." Philippians 2:12-13.

Ask God to confirm to you the personal court cases you can do on behalf of yourself and your family. The court cases will encompass any area that is out of order or doesn't have God's abundant life. Areas may include injustice, where people are stuck, or patterns of brokenness. When prayer alone seems not to yield results, the courts of heaven may be needed.

Proverbs 21:15 explains it well and says, "It is a joy for the just to do justice, but destruction will come to the workers of iniquity."

Journal thoughts here.

_____
_____
_____
_____
_____
_____
_____
_____
_____
_____
_____
_____
_____
_____

WHEN, WHERE & WHO IS QUALIFIED

WHEN

When can you do courts cases? Again, the answer is anytime. I keep notes on the cases I've done and write them in my journal as a record. There's a parable in Luke 18:1-8 that gives credence to getting God's attention. It's known as the "persistent widow". I know because of the authority of the believer that we're partnering with God through the courts. The Scripture in Luke tells us that we'll get His attention just because we're persistent.

WHERE

Where can you do court cases? 'Anywhere' is the answer. If I'm at home, I do them in my office. But I've literally done them in the car, at the store, in the bathroom, and everywhere else.

WHO

Ephesians 2:10 describes God giving us specific things to do; "For we are His workmanship, created in Christ Jesus for good works, which God prepared beforehand that we should walk in them." And Matthew 5:12 talks about our heavenly reward. "Rejoice and be exceedingly glad, for great is your reward in heaven."

In this section, we will talk about all the different reasons we can qualify to do a court case.

On whose behalf do we go into the courts? We go in for ourselves and for our family when things are out of order. In prayer, we can take things through the courts on behalf of those we pray for. We can take issues that need God's assistance or that are out of order, through the courts. A metron is the area or people group you're called to and the size of it. The seven mountains of cultural influence in the world are family, religion, education, media, entertainment, business, and government. Your metron will be in one (or two) of those areas and then be a specific size. For us to truly disciple nations for Jesus, we, as Kingdom Christians, will be in those mountains influencing the city, state, nation, or world for Christ. Size doesn't matter; what matters is that you do what you're assigned to do and do it well for Jesus. That's what He will look at and determine for your heavenly reward.

WHAT IS YOUR METRON?

You can do a courts case on behalf of you, your family, or your metron. The authority you have and how big your metron is will grow as you mature. Currently, you always have levels of authority for yourself, your neighborhood, your city, your state, and your nation. It is just a matter of how much authority you have. I always operate in all these areas and trust God to bring the result. I just know as I've grown, my authority and power have increased. If you're questioning how much authority you have, just be faithful with however much you have, and it'll increase.

For metron cases, it means we don't have generational sin. It has been taken care of through generational repentance. We don't have our own sin. If you're still acting in individual sin, go take care of that and then come back to the courts. We won't be perfect here on earth so if we do sin, we repent and take care of it with the Lord. What this means is, there's not sin that we engage in on a regular basis. If you're still sinning a lot, you need to grow up in the Lord and then come back to the courts.

Court cases can be confidential, especially metron cases. There are some I've done that only God and I know about because of the nature of them. I have permission to tell some of them from a teaching perspective, but otherwise I wouldn't tell. Always ask God before you share your courts cases.

You will do bigger metron cases as you grow. Some of you are already ready for them. Ask God if you're confused on this. Your metron will expand as you mature. In 2017, I wanted to do a court case on North Korea that they wouldn't attack the US. If you remember, that was very much in the news at that time. The Lord told me I couldn't do the case alone but could do it with Pamela if I asked her because she had the authority to do it. She was very kind to me, and we did the case together. After that, the news regarding North Korea settled down. I've done court cases alone on North Korea as it relates to the US since 2017 because I grew into the assignment.

Take a moment here and record what God says is your metron and the current size of it. Have faith in what He shows you because He cares more than you do that you accomplish your earthly mission well!

_____
_____
_____
_____
_____
_____
_____
_____
_____
_____
_____
_____
_____
_____
_____
_____
_____
_____

PARTNERING WITH GOD, OUR AUTHORITY ON EARTH

You can do a court case if you have "standing" in an area. If you've been hurt or affected by something, that's usually an example of standing. It gives you authority to do the case. You don't have to have standing to do a court case but if you do have standing, there's an authority you are walking in to do the case.

Psalm 24 talks about the clean hands and pure heart process and is another indicator for who can do a courts case. It's a good Psalm to read to understand this process.

Psalm 24 says, "The earth is the Lord's and all its fullness, the world and those who dwell therein. For He has founded it upon the seas and established it upon the waters. Who may ascend into the hill of the Lord? Or who may stand in His holy place? He who has clean hands and a pure heart, who has not lifted up his soul to an idol, nor sworn deceitfully. He shall receive blessing from the Lord, and righteousness from the God of his salvation. This is Jacob, the generation of those who seek Him, who seek Your face. Lift up your heads, O you gates! And be lifted up, you everlasting doors! And the King of glory shall come in. Who is this King of glory? The Lord strong and mighty, The Lord mighty in battle. Lift up your heads, O you gates! Lift up you everlasting doors! And the King of glory shall come in. Who is this King of glory? The Lord of hosts, He is the King of glory."

Is this you? Have you made a lifelong commitment to the Lord? Are you willing to do anything He says or asks of you with purity? Take a moment here to affirm your love and commitment to the Lord. He is truly good!

To walk faithfully with the Lord, we can't have unforgiveness or sin. We keep short accounts with the Lord if we do either of those. Sin and unforgiveness are what allows the enemy to come after you. It puts things back on the "train" board for the demons to grab hold of as an assignment.

I had a yearlong battle with Jezebel. It hurt! It was a painful process. It was full of the things that that spirit is full of. I felt hopeless, suicidal, and didn't want to go on. I had terrible dreams for a year. She also comes with sexual sin, but I didn't walk in that. At the end of the year, a friend of mine called and said, "Ding dong, the witch is dead." I knew God was talking about Jezebel. I knew who anchored the spirit in the natural, but it had more to do with the spiritual idea of it than interaction with the person. The next day we had a dramatic confirmation that the witch had certainly died.

A few months later, I was doing laundry and lamenting to God that I almost died, and it was so sad and hard how Jezebel had come after me for the entire year. I was whining to the Lord and feeling sorry for myself. He spoke then and said, 'Annie, you're looking at this wrong. She didn't come after you. I sent YOU after her!' Ahhhh! That changed everything! Then I was high fiving God! This was how it looked because of Psalm 24 and the clean hands and pure heart that I carry. Again, if you're not there yet, go take care of things so you can do the work God has for you.

If you've given your whole heart to God and given Him your life to do with as He pleases and assigns you to, He will use your life in the courts to bring about His will. If you haven't yet made that commitment to His Lordship, take some time right now to make the commitment and then journal what He says to you.

_____
_____
_____
_____
_____
_____
_____
_____
_____
_____
_____
_____
_____
_____
_____
_____
_____
_____
_____
_____

II.

WHERE TO BEGIN

COURTS POSTURE/PROTOCOLS FOR COURT WORK

Operating in the courts is a holy time because God is holy.

Childlike faith and trust in God give us our authority on earth. We are His sons and daughters here, and we have an open-door policy in heaven. We are always welcome and that's how we must see ourselves going into the courts. It's a true partnership with God. Ephesians 2:5-6 explains it by saying, (He) "made us alive together with Christ (by grace you have been saved), and raised us up together, and made us sit together in the heavenly places in Christ Jesus". This is our position now as we live on this earth.

The authority of the believer to bring heaven on earth explains our duty and right to authorize God's agenda on earth. We truly have the keys, and it is our responsibility to work with God to bring heaven to earth. Genesis 2:15 tells us our role, "Then the Lord God took the man and put him in the garden of Eden to tend it and keep it."

The heavenly courts are both regal and normal at the same time. Because of the Blood of Jesus, we have the authority of the believer. It is our right and duty to do court work with the Lord. Typically, we go into court respecting God, who is the judge. There is an honor we should expect to operate in. It also requires faith. Faith to understand if you don't see anything in the spirit or hear anything, that what you have just done happened and was important. You don't have to see or hear anything. You don't have to be a seer or feeler or anything in the spirit. If you do, great. If not, great, too. By faith you can know that God heard you. It's His justice system that you've operated in, and you'll see results. That means that everyone who is a believer can operate in the courts. That also means that every believer should operate in the courts of heaven. It's one of the ways we truly would bring heaven to earth if that were the case.

God is God. He determines how things work. Our duty to do court work gives us a partnership with God. It's how He designed us; to partner with Him. It does not, however, give us control. We don't get to control how things look on earth. The answer to prayer may not look like we thought it would, but if we trust God, it'll work out for good. I've seen about fifty percent of the work happen immediately; the other fifty percent takes a process. You will see many miracles. Some of the miracles come instantly, especially if it's for you. Some of the miracles will need some additional court work if they're for family or other people. However it looks, if you pursue God's justice, you will get it.

Our lives are a balance between walking in the fear of the Lord and the love of the Lord. If you walk in the middle of both of those you won't get into sloppy grace or the misunderstanding of the Father not being good. He is absolutely good and absolutely the judge. We are so loved, and are so His children, and we are so beholden to Him.

Deuteronomy 8:6 says, "Therefore you shall keep the commandments of the Lord your God, to walk in His ways and to fear Him."

Job 28:28 says, "And to man He said, 'Behold, the fear of the Lord, that is wisdom, and to depart from evil is understanding."

Zephaniah 3:17 (my favorite verse in the Bible!) says, "The Lord your God in your midst, the Mighty One, will save; He will rejoice over you with gladness, He will quiet you with His love, He will rejoice over you with singing."

Can you feel the love from that last Scripture? It is the balance of walking in the fear of the Lord and the love of the Lord. Take a few minutes and journal here anything the Lord wants to tell you.

_____

_____

_____

_____

_____

_____

_____

_____

PERSONAL COURT PROCEDURE

First, you need to go through the process of generational repentance explained earlier and then personally through the courts of heaven. Once the generational repentance is done, you're ready to go into courts for yourself. This is a good place in the book to do the personal courts session because a lot of the next part of the book talks about metron court cases. If you're ready, follow along. If not, skip this section and come back when you're ready. The papers start on p. 62. Turn to the papers now and follow along both there and here.

We go through four courts in the initial session. This should take a little over an hour. Once you're finished with your personal court sessions, you'll change from defense in the courts to offense in the courts and be ready to expand into other sessions for your personal life. You will also be ready for your metron court sessions. After your personal session, your "train board" is wiped clean and the demons have nothing left to grab onto.

All the included documents pages are highlighted in bold and italicized so you'll know which page to use.

Before we begin, I pray aloud the Opening Prayer (A). I can tell when a person has either a high call or has things unresolved because I may pick up warfare a few days or a week ahead of time. They're usually feeling the warfare, too. If that's the case, I'll pray the preparation prayer at that time and then again before the session. That makes the warfare stop or makes it manageable for me. Either way, the person is getting free!

I have the client sign the Petitions of Divorce from the Bloodline before we begin. These sheets were in the book, Silencing the Accuser. This officially removes the contract with the demonic and includes the marriage to Jehovah. Wherever the person was in their life, it's an official end and beginning. Then we're ready to move into court work.

REPENTENTANCE AND THE MERCY COURT

The first is the Mercy Court (B). Mercy requires repentance. For the first fifty people I took through the courts, I did an initial interview with them for what was in their individual families. This took about an hour. I started to see people had similar issues, so I made a list of everything people said. To shorten the time for future sessions, I gave people the list and asked them to just repent for whatever was highlighted by God. People didn't know what their families had done, and didn't want to miss anything, so everyone said everything. I named the sheet "Master Sheet". So, in the Mercy court, we take the Mercy Court Master sheet (C) and say everything there. In the mercy court it feels heavy in the beginning as the sin is confessed. Some of the confessions are redundant, yet if the sins no longer exist—once sins are confessed—like the Bible says in Hebrews 8:12, the somberness of the courts wouldn't feel that way. "For I will be merciful to their unrighteousness, and their sins and their lawless deeds I will remember no more." So, I know some of the sins have not yet been confessed despite how comprehensive the generational repentance was. Once the confession is through, the atmosphere is a lot lighter, and joy comes.

After the confession of sin, we look into the spiritual realm to see which of our ancestors in the great cloud of witnesses shows up to give testimony. If you're not very familiar with this, it usually comes as an impression or a knowing or even seeing on the screen of your imagination. Just relax and trust God in this.

This can be a powerful time. Everyone sees people. There must be a grace from God on the process for people to see/know even if they don't normally see or know. It can give people comfort to know who is fighting in heaven for us. I've seen miscarried or aborted children show up in this spot and grandparents and parents that people hadn't known if they were saved. Sometimes it's very emotional. Other times, it's not. I think one of the benefits of seeing people is it can strengthen us in life as we run our race. It makes us aware that we have the baton and that our ancestors depend on us to run well.

I have a friend who told me when she did this part in her court case, she saw her two great grandmothers clapping and cheering her on and thanking her for caring for the family so well. She didn't know them in life but knew who they were here. Their enthusiastic response showed her she was part of an extended team. She no longer felt alone in her court work.

After that you can ask God for what you'd like back for justice and for what was stolen which will now be returned.

Then ask Him to end the case. If it is finished, you will see or know it's finished, see a gavel going down, see a signature, or anything that would indicate it's finished. If it's not, you'll be reminded of something else to repent from or ask for. Once the mercy court is over, you'll feel a lot lighter and more joyful. I usually don't ever go back into the mercy court unless God specifically directs me. It's a one and done court. Once the repentance has happened, unless new sin has occurred, you don't have to go back to the mercy court.

PURSUING RESTORATION THROUGH THE APPELLATE COURT

The Appellate Court (D) is next. Appellate means to appeal. This is where you will appeal the injustices that have occurred and ask God for your promises to come to pass. It's a court where both negative things can be stopped and positive things can happen. In general, for future work, I do most of my court work in this court. It's fast and easy. We always use the appellate court sheet for the first time and the master sheet for the things that can be in this court. In subsequent times, if it is easier to use the sheet, you can use it. If you don't want to use it and feel comfortable stating your case, you can do it that way. I personally don't use the sheet anymore. I direct my cases to the judge in my own words.

Court work has more to do with understanding that it's God's justice system and your faith in it, than what you say or don't say. If you're respectful, God wants your faith in His system to be built and to grow.

For the appellate court, you say aloud the judgments you want reversed and the promises you want to have come to pass. You get the judgments and the promises from the lists you made about your family prior to going into court. Then you use the Appellate Court Master Sheet (E) for any personal injustices and for your family's injustices. In the next part, you ask God for what measures you will accept in return. It really is a time of great redemption. This part feels hopeful and joyful. You may feel upset by injustices against you and your family as you contend for justice and restitution, but you can be confident God is going to act on your behalf.

THE TROPHY ROOM IN HELL

The Trophy Room in Hell (F) is the next step in generational restoration. This room is where the enemy, who has taken your generational blessings, mantles, finances, and other callings puts them. This can be quite grand in getting your things back. I've seen dreaming come back because God's justice comes. It can totally change everything in your family once your things are back. I took one of my friends through the courts and she had the most dramatic testimony. Everything in her life rapidly changed after the courts. She remarried, her finances changed for the better, her career took off, and everything in her children's lives changed for the better, too. It's not merely symbolic that you're getting things back from the trophy room. It's also literal and the more that's in there, the more change for the better that you'll see.

First, we freeze and silence the trophy room so that we can go in without a battle. Then we say aloud the things we know are in there, as well as the Master Sheet for Trophy Room (G) of things that may be in there. We give everything we picked up to Jesus. He will give it back to us as we can steward it. Typically, we get about a third to half of our stuff immediately. When you are done, ask Jesus if there's anything else in there for you and listen to what He says. About half the time, there's still something in there. Once He clears it for you, please unfreeze and un-silence the trophy room. There have been times that I've gone back to the trophy room at God's direction. Otherwise, I consider it done and count on Jesus to tell me if I need to go get something out for myself or family.

THE COURTS OF TIMES AND SEASONS

The final court is the Court of Times and Seasons (H). It is very easy to do, and God does the work in the courts. What it does is it calibrates people's timing with heaven's timing after all the work we did. In this court, we ask God for the angels to recalibrate the timing. Then we watch it happen. Usually, it's a very quick work, taking just a few minutes. We typically see clocks adjust to 12 o'clock. There are many clocks on hand for different things in the person's life. Normally, I see a grandfather clock that readjusts. That's the clock for the entire family getting reset.

At the end of the session, I pray aloud the Sealing Prayer (I). This sets the work and doesn't allow it to be adjusted. It also allows for no warfare after the work is done.

Take some time now and make any notes to compile the results of your personal court case. Listen to the Lord for any further instructions.

_____
_____
_____
_____
_____
_____
_____
_____
_____
_____
_____
_____
_____
_____
_____

The Authority of the Believer

Jesus, after his resurrection, declared that all authority in heaven and on earth had been given to him (Matthew 28:18). He then commissioned believers to make disciples, baptizing and teaching them (Matthew 28:19-20). This commission implies that believers are empowered to act on Jesus' behalf and to exercise his authority in the world. This authority is not passive; it requires active participation and faith from the believer. Believers can resist the devil, rebuke sickness, and operate in other spiritual gifts. This authority is not a license to do whatever one pleases but a responsibility to advance God's will on Earth. This is the assignment and the authority we have on this earth. This is what gives you the authority and the responsibility to do your court cases.

III.

MOVING TO OFFENSE

HOW TO DO METRON COURT CASES

This is the million-dollar question. How do we do the courts? I want you to be in the courts daily and weekly for your metron. That does not mean you have to be an expert in the courts before you go in. I want to give permission for you and God to do things whatever way is easiest for you. I really believe what He's calling you to do, you can do easily with His help and gain lots of fruit with your efforts.

Now that you're done with your major personal court session, you may do metron court cases. In general, here are the steps.

1. Repent for known and unknown sin.
2. Forgive them and ask God to forgive them.
3. Ask God to judge any demonic spirits associated with this issue you have brought to the courts
4. Ask for God's solution for the event and for the person/people.
5. "Listen" through the ways God speaks about the things He "says" for anything else. If so, do or say whatever He says.
6. Thank Him for His courts.

The following is an example of an accepted way of doing a bigger metron case. (1) I will forgive the people who have sinned and (2) I will repent on their behalf for sinning for each sin. This is identificational repentance, just like Daniel repented for the nation of Israel in Daniel 9. It's a good book in the Bible to read to understand our role as intercessors. Steps 1 and 2 are basically the mercy court. This can take a few minutes or longer. My court case for the abominations of the Obama administration that I'll discuss later in the book was nine pages of actions that I'd identified and listed. It took a while to list all the sins and repent for them. You should feel both sorry that the sins were committed and happy that God is bringing justice. (3) I'll then ask God to judge the demonic spirits behind the actions and to judge the actions. You don't ask God to judge the person. This is important. Through the courts we're

31

asking God to judge the enemy and not judge the people. Through our court cases people may end up with consequences for their actions but it is God who decides that and not us doing the deciding. (4) Then I'll ask God for His solutions. I may submit prophetic words and Scriptures. (5) Then I'll listen for God's instructions. (6) And thank Him for His courts.

If you follow these steps, you'll always be right. A lot of times once sin has been confessed in an area, I'll skip steps and merely make a declaration of God's solution. I can "feel" or "know" by using spiritual discernment which way it needs to go. If I'm not sure, I'll do the steps above. Do however it works for you. I always acknowledge in some way that I know I'm in His courts. Whether I say, "I'm coming into Your courts" or "I'm in Your court" or "Thank You for Your courts" it's an acknowledgement that I'm in court.

Write any questions you have for the Lord here and listen to Him for the answers.

_____
_____
_____
_____
_____
_____
_____
_____
_____
_____
_____
_____
_____
_____
_____
_____
_____
_____

I don't always do the above steps. Sometimes I'll literally announce the problem and/or solution and leave it at that. If I feel that the courts work listed in steps 1-3 has been done already, the courts can be simple. I will discern how much court work to do. God speaks through discernment and through our knowing and feeling. Not knowing and feeling in the emotional sense but knowing and feeling in the spiritual sense. If you haven't developed your discernment yet, you may ask God to hear His response or see what He shows you. Either way, He will "speak" to you in one of the 4 primary ways He "speaks" (seeing, hearing, feeling, knowing) to help you in court.

For example, in January of 2022, I did a court case for not having another worldwide pandemic. It took about 5 seconds to do the court case. I said, "Thank You, Lord, for your courts. We will not have another worldwide or national pandemic. Thank You." It was a complete court case in and of itself. I believe we won't have another worldwide pandemic because of the court case I did. I think the people behind the scenes had planned another one (monkey pox) and it just fizzled out and came to nothing.

Do you understand the authority of the Believer? Do you know that what we allow on earth happens and what we don't allow doesn't happen. We are the kings of King Jesus and our ruling here matters. Matthew 18:18 says, "Assuredly, I say to you, whatever you bind on earth will be bound in heaven, and whatever you loose on earth will be loosed in heaven." This ruling that we do happens in the courts of heaven. This ruling is important because much of what happens or doesn't happen actually depends on how believers' rule.

I am called to the political mountain. What mountain are you sensing you are called to? Your court cases, no matter what the mountain, are important for the world and therefore, for you to do. We need everyone who reads this book to get activated and play their role.

In January 2020, I read a book that changed my life. It made everything I knew, in part, come together. It was The Killing of Uncle Sam: The Demise of the United States of America by Rodney Howard-Browne and Paul L. Williams. Later I read the sequel, Killing the Planet: How a Financial Cartel Doomed Mankind. Neither book is light reading, but it put together the enemy's plan against our nation and how much freedom we had already lost. I was scheduled to preach at a church, and I told the Lord the believers didn't know the terrible things the pedophiles and Luciferian leaders had done in our world, and I asked Him if I should tell them. His response was clear as day and surprised me. He said very casually, "Nah, tell them what comes next. I'm removing all the evil leaders in the mountains. My believers haven't been able to serve in the mountains because the tops of them have been full of pedophiles and global crooks. Tell them to get ready to serve in the mountains because I'm putting them in the mountains at all levels. It's almost time to disciple nations for Me."

Then one morning in April 2023, the Lord spoke and said, "It's time to disciple nations". He has cleaned out almost all the mountains and the believers need to take their places. If this is you, please move forward with what the Lord has shown you. We have a lot to do to change this world for Jesus. Curriculum needs to be rewritten. The food industry needs the poisons to be removed. Entertainment needs to be changed. There is a lot in every mountain of influence to be changed for Jesus. It'll take each of us doing our part as well as all the court cases that enable us to do it. If this part isn't quickening your spirit for what you can do, spend some time with Jesus and He will show you!

VICTORIOUS ESCHATOLOGY

This segment is important to help clarify where we are on the timeline of God's big picture. It is not the time for the rapture or the end time. For whatever reason, the enemy wants to shorten the timeline between now and when Jesus returns, but God is glorified by our discipling His nations. If you think the rapture is soon, you're not doing the part of the timeline that God needs us to do. We need to build now. It's not the time to run away. My Jesus paid a big price on the Cross and isn't coming back for a weak bride who needs rescuing. We will become a bride without spot or wrinkle (Ephesians 5:27), and the nations will look like Jesus.

Years ago, I read Victorious Eschatology co-authored by Dr. Harold Eberle and Dr. Martin Trench. The book is described as "A biblically based, optimistic view of the future. Along with a historic perspective, they present a clear understanding of Matthew 24, the book of Revelation, and other key passages about the events that precede the return of Jesus Christ. Satan is not going to take over this world. Jesus Christ is Lord, and He will reign until every enemy is put under His feet." If this is already your world view, then you're ready for the court cases that clean up this world and make it like His. If it's not, I encourage you to read this book. It is very Scriptural and presents the case that matches what I know about Jesus. It doesn't take the enemy out of the picture, but it makes believers bigger and more powerful until the nations are discipled, and Jesus comes back for a victorious bride.

I don't know what happens in the book of Revelation scriptures, but I know we are not in that time frame now. Now is the time to disciple the nations. I expect that God will reveal revelation on that time frame as we get closer. I do not expect it to be in my lifetime because of prophetic words I've received and other things that God has told me. I have had dreams of the supernatural things we will do when the end times draw near. We will have supernatural abilities like running faster than traffic and teleporting around the world through portals. We will need those abilities then because of what we will do for God. That time, however, is not now. Now is the time to disciple nations and our attention should be on that.

If you've had a lot of warfare in your life and are feeling discouraged, please understand the courts will not only help even the playing field for you but put you on top. We were made to be victorious, and Jesus helps us with that through the courts. If you're tired, ask God for more energy and rejuvenation. God will bring a blessing of energy, rejuvenation, and a victory for you that energizes you!

Take some time here to journal what God wants to show you about your life and your legacy for the generations. Ask God, "What legacy do you want me to leave? How can I disciple my family, state, or nation? How can I bring your kingdom to my mountain of influence?"

_____
_____
_____
_____
_____
_____
_____
_____
_____
_____
_____
_____
_____

EXAMPLES OF COURT CASES AND SEASONS

When I did a Rothschild court case, I knew before I did it that an entire case would have to be done on the entire political and economic system. The day before, I happened to be listening to a podcast which I thought would be political in nature. Instead, the head of the podcast did a political court case with three intercessors. I joined in, listened to the entire thing, and added my agreement to it. At the end, I had the fleeting thought that I could now do the Rothschild case, but it was just a thought. The next day, I did a Rothschild court case which I explain later in this book.

We must trust God for the outcome. About fifty percent of the cases I have done start a process, while fifty percent of the cases get a victory immediately. God oversees which needs to occur.

For example, in January 2022, I did a court case that all bioweapons' labs in the world would be exposed and destroyed. I did not have knowledge that there were bioweapons labs worldwide. The Lord asked me to do the case, so I did it. The court case was literally 5 seconds long. I didn't feel it needed to be more than that. "Lord, I come into your courts. All bioweapons' labs in the world will be exposed and destroyed. Thank you." The fact that the declaration was made in the courts system in heaven is why there was immediate fruit.

At the time, I didn't have natural knowledge of the labs except for the Wuhan, China one. Then Russia invaded Ukraine. About a month later, I was listening to a podcast where they mentioned that in Ukraine there were a minimum of eleven bioweapons labs and the Russian government focused their invasion on bioweapons that were targeted at the Slavic people of Russia. The Lord tapped me on the shoulder and said, "This is the result of your bioweapons labs court case." I was stunned. Russia invaded Ukraine because I did a court case? Russia invaded Ukraine because of Ukraine's bioweapons labs that targeted Russian people. The latest count showed over fifty bioweapons' labs in Ukraine. The work we do in the spirit is very important to what happens in the natural. It'll also come out that there are many bioweapons' labs in Taiwan. We will see what happens there. This is an example of where a court case that I did started a process— the removal of bioweapons' labs.

Sometimes we see action and sometimes we see quiet. When I did the court case for North Korea, I didn't see anything happen in 2017, except that the entire region quieted down. There may have been things that happened behind the scenes that only the leaders saw. Either way, God gave us the authority of the believer to rule nations here on earth.

When doing court cases, if we're asking God for help, we don't need to do repentance/forgiveness or ask Him to judge the demonic spirits. We just ask Him for help in an area. For example, my husband, at one point, was the director of operations at a candy company. They were having hiring troubles for an engineer and kitchen staff. I went into the courts and asked God for help in those two areas. That is literally all I did, taking less than ten seconds for the entire case. The next day, they had new kitchen help come in and then quickly hired an engineer who has been there for over a year and is a good fit. God answered the court case very quickly.

Because the courts are God's way of doing things, I go into the courts. I still pray, but some things may have taken a lot more prayer and time to change. And if I take something into the courts, I don't pray about it. We don't intercede in the courts. It's not an intercession place. We submit our case and leave it in God's hands. We state solutions that we need and leave it up to God. We ask for healing and we ask for wisdom.

Take some time with God right now and write down court cases you need to do personally for things that concern you and your family. (In the next journaling area, you'll write your metron cases.)

_____
_____
_____
_____
_____
_____
_____
_____
_____
_____

Now take some time with God and write down metron court cases you need to do.

_____
_____
_____
_____
_____
_____
_____
_____
_____
_____
_____
_____
_____
_____
_____
_____
_____

The following are many examples of court cases I've done, along with tips I've learned along the way. It'll help you see how diverse the courts of heaven are and how much we can impact the world with the courts of heaven.

Before I knew about God's system of the courts, my mom spent four weeks in the hospital, three and a half of them were in a coma before she died. That was very hard and not a grace period. After that experience, I decided I wanted our family to have a graced dying process, one where the medical system isn't involved, and without all the costs. Through court work, my dad was completely independent and then spent a week in the hospital before he died. I didn't want either parent to die in their home because of resale of the house. My dad dying in the hospital was better and had more grace. I didn't want any family members to go into assisted living or a nursing home. That was important to me for the dignity of the family member and for the passing on of the inheritance. I did more court work and then my father-in-law died in his bed completely healthy. That was full of grace by not involving the hospital at all. My father-in-law surprised us by dying, so some would say that wasn't grace. You must decide what works for your family and present it in court that way.

On another occasion a year ago, I was in the laundry room turning on the washer to wash clothes. It made a noise, but nothing came on the screen, and despite my turning of the knobs, it would not work. My daughter had used the washer the night before, but it refused to work for me. I asked God's presence to come for healing and prayed healing over the washer and commanded anything not of God to leave and then tried to turn it on. It did not work. I tried by praying two more times. Finally, I did a short court case. I told God I was in the courts for my washer, I asked for Him to judge anything demonic associated with it, and for the washer to work. The entire court case took about five seconds. Then I turned the washer on, and it worked. This example really improved my understanding and appreciation for the courts. The courts are where the justice of God happens.

My husband drove an eleven-year-old Prius to work and home. It's a great car for that kind of driving. The engine light came on and the car started making noises. It needed some repair work, but the repair was going to cost more than the car was worth, so we did a court case for a supernatural solution in our timing. God helps in these situations. The car lasted two more years before we sold it.

We can still decree a matter, and it'll happen because that's in the Bible. But I have found if I ask God in court for a solution it'll happen. The courts are a way of partnering with God. We ask in court for God's will to be done because we know He will do it. We're not praying "if it's Your will". We know it's His will.

The area I stay away from for the courts is marriage if people are not yet married. The reason I do that is because people have free will. They get to choose their partner or not choose their partner in deciding whether or not to get married. Even if God has given prophetic words about it, people still have a choice. If two people are married, I will take a case into court for them to be successful in marriage. One thing I do for people who are dating, though, is take it into court and ask God if there is a reason it should end, and if so, that He will expose things and bring a quick resolution. This saves the dating couple the trouble of a longer process.

You can use the courts in intercession areas, but it's not intercession in the courts. Can you understand the difference here? Anything I prayed about before on anyone's behalf, I take into the courts for them and ask for God's solution. Those areas come very quickly. If they want a full breakthrough, they need to do the generational work. I've had cases where I've asked God for healing. I've done the forgiveness and repentance for the person in this area. I've seen people get healed from this. I've also seen people not get healed in a situation. It could be because I didn't repent of what was on the board that the enemy was grabbing onto. It could be because they had free will and wanted to go be with Jesus. That's one of those mysteries that I may or may not know until I get to heaven.

I've had two dreams where God has shown me that using the courts for a business area makes any business successful. Even businesses that have poor products and other problems. I don't mean poor in integrity issues but in not being great ideas for a market. God always wants to help people and companies become more like Jesus and sometimes that takes a process that the courts can help in.

When my husband worked for an upscale real estate company in California, the company built an $8 million home for resale. After a year, it still hadn't sold. We'd prayed for it to sell over the year, but it hadn't sold. My husband asked me to take the house sale into the courts of heaven. I did, and the house sold a few days later. It probably wouldn't have sold without the courts. Whatever the issue was with the house, the courts addressed it.

In another instance, the company was being sued by another businessman for malfeasance. The entire situation was convoluted and was making business stressful. My husband took the issue to the courts of heaven where God said to him, "I wanted to solve this issue for you, so thank you for bringing it into the courts." We were astounded by God's response. The court case in the natural was dropped that week and the other businessman walked away from the malfeasance situation.

In general, if you don't understand the geopolitical issues of nations, don't take them into the courts. You may not be on the right side of the case. I believe if you or I are not on the right side of the case, God just doesn't answer it. I know a lot more about nations than I did five years ago, but I can still get startled. The Russia/Ukraine war was a good example of this.

Some court cases already have a solution. Some court cases are in process. I had a dream in February 2017 where the Father asked me to do a court case about the encroachment former President Obama did to President Trump. At the time, I didn't know anything about the encroachment and didn't feel confident enough to do the case myself. I asked several people to do the case with me, but it didn't work out to do the case that way. Finally, in February 2019, I did the case myself. I researched and wrote out nine pages of sins and political encroachments. The case was very detailed, and I listed each item as a sin and repented for it. At the end, I asked God to judge the spirits behind the actions and judge the actions. The aftereffects of that case are not yet publicly available.

In January 2017, the Lord told my friend, Pamela, that there were listening devices implanted in the White House walls and ceiling. This was before President Trump said anything or anything had been in the media about it. On inauguration day, she and I did a court case together and asked God to make the devices known and remove them. About a week later, it came out through President Trump about the listening devices, and they were removed.

Our breakthrough came immediately after the financial court case I did that removed the Rothschild, Rockefeller, and unrighteous Kennedys from the US that I will talk about later in the book. It's always possible that you're a Hannah crying out for a baby and God is crying out for a nation's salvation. Some of your breakthroughs will come after the nation's breakthrough comes. So don't be discouraged or stop doing the courts if your breakthrough hasn't come yet.

My daughter moved back from ministry school to North Carolina. It seemed the next eight months were a waiting period as she found a job, worked, and lived at home. Suddenly, she met her future husband. As we talked to him, he told us how he'd had God encounters and healings in the previous year and was a different man than he was the year before. I believe the courts cases we did for him a few years prior to their meeting is what enabled all the breakthrough even though we didn't know it was happening, other than the faith of the heavenly court system.

A former student, and now friend, called yesterday with a court's testimony. Both of her parents got diagnosed with cancer last year. They were going through medical treatments and were really struggling financially. She set up a fund for people to donate to help them but very little was coming into it and they had large medical bills. She called a minister friend of ours whom I had taken through and taught the courts to and asked for help praying through the situation. The friend suggested they take it into the courts. So, they did. Right after that, the donation fund gained $20,000 and the hospital wrote them a letter saying they'd canceled all the bills. The mom said that her daughter working with God really answered their prayers. It was a true miracle that built everyone's faith.

I also did a US health case regarding chemicals and gluten in our wheat system. I did an entire court case on all the issues that I knew about regarding health and diet in the American system. I know those things will change. Thus far, I don't have any specific knowledge of the changes, but they are coming. That case was very involved, and I followed the detailed steps I gave on metron cases. This court case was done in 2022. Since then, Robert F. Kennedy, Jr. was appointed to President Trump's cabinet as Health and Human Services Secretary. RFK Jr. has recently talked about the poisons in our food system so there's already movement in this situation. Robert F. Kennedy, Jr. gave an interview where he said he prayed and asked God over the past nineteen years for this opportunity to clean up the United States food and agricultural system. Thank You, Jesus for answering this prayer for our nation.

In general, if I have done an involved court case or participated in one or know that one has been done, then I can take issues into the courts regarding that subject, and it can take a few seconds or less than a minute. That's something you'll have to work with God about. If you don't know, you'll have to do the elaborate court case. If you look back through your life, you will see the Lord has already set you up to do courts cases to set the nation and world free.

The Lord has given me five nations to steward in my life. They are the US, France, Italy, Israel, and Russia. I've prayed for them over the years. A lot. But thus far, I've done one court case freeing them from the central banking system. I'm sure there will be more but at this time my focus is on the US.

Victory in court has more to do with you understanding your authority and understanding the power of the courts, than what you say or do in court. So be confident!

I did a court case in mid-March of 2022 for the federal mask mandates. I personally only ever wore one when I went into Costco, and I had had enough of the face masks! I gave a timeline for them to be phased out by the end of April. I know some things take time, but I knew the timeline was based on my authority. So, I gave a timeline. The federal mask mandates finished by the end of April. Thank God!

As I write the testimonies of what God has done, I am so thankful. And I know that each one of you readers needs to see what area you're interested in and get to work on court cases. Some of you will have different interests than mine. It takes a small army of people to bring heaven to earth!

From the first class I taught in Redding, California, in 2022, I spoke to one of my students in class and told her she needed to be responsible for California's water system. The rain, the snow, the lakes, the rivers, and the storage of it. It was a word of knowledge that God gave me. She nodded during class and after class, said she and her husband had gotten a word from Cindy Jacobs that they were responsible for the California water system but had no idea how to do that. After the teaching, she knew exactly what to do. These last years the lakes in California filled up! She's not done, but so much has been accomplished. Since my original writing of this book, more has happened in this situation. Things have been put into place for a resolution to California's water problem. The drought has ended. The fires in Southern California have brought California's water problems to national awareness. People in the federal government are aware of the problems and the dynamics involved.

Another student was responsible for the California election system, and she started work in Shasta County, California, both speaking at the county Board of Supervisors meetings and doing court work. That's a fraudulent system that needs unraveling and so much has already been accomplished. That student is in her 80s and is really enjoying working with God on such big issues. This is our job as God's people.

One student did a court case in 2023 about the media in her area publishing only liberal material generally and propagandizing in the extreme. They were not publishing conservative material at all. She wanted the conservative voice to be heard so she did a court case regarding that view. She didn't see anything happen for the next 18 months, but she knew she'd taken it before the King and thought He'd do something. 18 months later, a man came to see ten of the conservatives in the area. He told them that twenty years before in Florida, a group of them had started an online conservative news source, made the advertising half off the normal rate, and began to publish with these conservatives writing news articles. It didn't take long before they put the liberal newspaper out of business. He said the current newspaper was struggling financially and if they did what the Florida people had done, the newspaper didn't have long and would be out of business. Before the court case, they didn't have the strategy for what to do and God sent them a man to tell them the strategy. Our court cases will take both going to court and action afterwards to bring about God's purposes. You may be playing the intercessor role and doing the court cases. You may be taking subsequent action. Both are necessary for this next season in God's roles for us on earth.

Another student got a prophetic word that God wanted to promote him at his company in a faster amount of time than the normal schedule for those who are doing well. Assuming he was doing well, he was due for a promotion in 12-24 months. About two months after the word, for different reasons, four out of the team of five left their roles. He was the only one left to do the work of the entire team. His boss did a little of the work to help him out but the majority of it was left to him. He worked hard and somehow got the work done well. He did that for three months and then talked to his boss about a promotion. His boss told him he had tried to get him promoted that month, but the human resources division said no. The student thought about it and then did a court case taking the earlier prophetic word about the early promotion into court. The next month, the leadership team, without his knowledge, put the promotion through. The courts of heaven are a large component of getting God's will through into the regular world. Whether it is the demonic or people not working with the will of God, the courts of heaven addresses it to bring God's will forth.

One student works as a teacher in a childcare facility. She's been there less than a year and doesn't have any natural authority because she's not in management, but she has spiritual authority. Parents were complaining about another teacher in another classroom. They felt their children weren't safe, but the teacher had worked there for over a decade and management hadn't addressed the situation in all that time. My student was quite concerned about the children, so she took the case into the courts of heaven. It was a short case where she went into the court, thanked God for courts, and said she was bringing the safety and wellbeing of the children into the courts and asking

God for His solution. She didn't address the teacher at all, just the children's safety. Later that week, management brought the teacher into the office for a chat, took the teacher to another facility to show her how they did that classroom, and the teacher came back and made adjustments. The children are all much happier and safer. To me, this is a miracle in the workplace. This is how we bring heaven to earth especially when we don't have natural authority to make changes.

Some court cases feel more important compared to a court case I just did but God really loves us and cares about every area of our lives. My husband and I were out on the boat with our daughter and son in law. We had enjoyed the day and were ready to go back to shore. Joe went to pull the anchor in and found he couldn't move it. It was stuck in something and was completely immobile. Our son in law tried to move it and couldn't move it, either. Joe got the knife out and was going to cut the rope and leave the anchor in the lake. In the meantime, I did a court case. I very simply asked God to send an angel to unstick the anchor on the lake floor. My daughter said to her dad, "Wait. Mom just did a court case. Try to move the anchor now before you cut it." So, my son in law went back to the rope and pulled it right up and in the boat. I did the court case because I understand that God works like this and this is how heaven is involved in our lives. I knew God would respond and I gave Him the glory and worship for the miracle.

If I had prayed for the anchor to come up, nothing may have happened. But taking it into the courts of heaven, I got a very quick answer that the enemy has no recourse to. Justice happens immediately. If you're apostolic and a builder, please understand the partnering with someone who understands the courts of heaven. This is how we bring heaven to earth. Whether it's something simple like an anchor or something complicated like not having another pandemic or nuclear war, God cares and responds.

One student is called to the family mountain and after doing court work had a breakthrough in her family. That really cures the heart!

In a class in 2022, as a group, we did a courts session on the supply issues the US was facing. At the time, stores were out of things and the system looked to be in trouble with shipping containers waiting off the coast to be unloaded. At the end of that session, we said no supply chain issues, no lack. Which is what happened. It all quickly worked out.

I've done court cases on not having another pandemic, no cyber pandemics, no financial collapse, no civil war, no great reset of the central banking type, no social credit system, no vaccine passports, and our country not being hurt by artificial intelligence.

I also have a "no major nuclear weapons going off in my lifetime" declaration. I will not allow that.

When you know who you are in God and know whose you are, you can bring health and safety to this earth. We do this through the courts cases we do. By not allowing the darkness to reign, people can get to know Christ and live for Him.

Courts can be a vehicle to solve problems on defense and move forward on offense. Defense consists of getting rid of "the stack of documents".

Some of the things that we've dealt with in healing relationships include the pattern of thinking that you know what someone is thinking or their motive. Despite instructions that there's no way to know what a person is thinking, the pattern won't stop until court work for the pattern happens, then more communication can occur between relationships and the pattern will stop. That can really change relationships.

God's justice system is his courts. It's how He set things to work to bring heaven to earth. That's a prayer we pray regularly. God help us bring heaven to earth. The courts in heaven are a primary way this works for us. There's a reason that God released the courts throughout the body of Christ at the same time. People all over the world suddenly had the revelation. It wasn't just one stream that had it. It was all over the world. When God releases revelation like that, we need to pay attention. He doesn't want this to be a temporary thing for a while and then we go onto the next. He wants this to be a primary way His believers operate.

When God releases revelation, especially so widespread that it can't be considered revelation of one stream, we often find the scriptures come alive as a secondary experience. It turns out the scriptures are full of the courts of heaven. This can be a hard experience for teachers who like revelation to come from the scriptures first. If you're having trouble with the courts of heaven scripturally, I suggest you meditate on the scriptures included at the back of this book. This list is just an example of some of the scriptures. Many more are throughout the Bible.

THE MISSING PIECES

I began to take people through the courts as my church kept referring people to me. People were experiencing major breakthroughs in areas that had—prior to the court's session—proved ineffectual. They'd fasted; they'd prayed and done everything they knew to do. These were God's people who had prophetic words about the breakthroughs, yet they knew despite their best efforts, they were receiving no breakthrough.

I saw one couple who had been unemployed for eight months and had gone through their savings. They were desperate and couldn't seem to get a job as if their lives depended on it. And their lives did depend on them getting a job. Prior to the appointment, they went through the generational repentance I recommended and came to me with the two lists I'd requested. The first list was any and all areas of family injustices or problems. The second list was everything they'd ever felt God promised them personally or through a prophetic word. The husband had his phone silenced as we went through the courts. As we finished and came back to the table, he turned on his phone and there was a voicemail requesting an interview! God answered their petition immediately, and he got that job. Another thing they'd requested God's assistance for was that they had two brothers who had never been able to buy a house. Both brothers bought houses a couple of months later.

Those stories gave me such hope and such faith that the God who answers prayers was breathing on this courts system of His. I saw so many answers to prayer. We saw a lung tumor disappear. We saw many financial miracles, marriages, children, prodigals return, and pregnancies.

I saw an entire family change. They all loved the Lord but were stuck. They had grown children and grandchildren. They all suffered with different issues that didn't seem related. They had all the prophetic promises but not much fruit. After the generational repentance, so many things in each of them changed. It was fascinating to watch. These people really loved the Lord and couldn't get a breakthrough of God's promises until they went into His courts.

I took a woman through the courts for her business. While she was repenting, I asked the Lord if it was really this easy. We weren't doing much in my natural opinion. My dad had been a circuit court judge in real life before he passed and would bring home his cases in file folders that looked like an accordion. They'd expand to hold all the documents for the case. The picture the Lord showed me was, as we repented from the sin by saying the word or phrase, the angels would take a case file and fill it in with all the details needed. Heaven did the heavy lifting. I was so encouraged by how easy the courts system was. We were supposed to operate there and trust God to do the heavy lifting. We didn't need a law degree or much experience.

By getting rid of the generational sin, keeping a short account where we forgive those who offend us, and repenting of anything we do, our lives can really be a lot simpler. The board of sin can really be empty. We can then go forward with lots of momentum to build God's kingdom and disciple the nations.

I think this is a key piece that has been missing for people. How many people do we know that, as soon as they stand up for God, have then had all kinds of hardships and battles? It's not supposed to be like that. The people we could see that were able to build without all kinds of warfare simultaneously would be families that were 5 and 6 generations saved. And yet, even though those families could also have major battles, the enemy could not take them out.

When I was teaching, the students who were first or second generation saved had many more problems than the students who were third or more generations saved. I would see this regardless of how long people had been saved or how old they were. What would change that situation was generational repentance. That was the major game changer for people.

Before I required students to do the generational repentance, I had two students in the same class that, when they got close to me, my Holy Spirit alarm would go off. He would shout, "Witch! Witch! Witch!" That was alarming for sure. I approached both of those students privately and asked each of them to do the generational repentance. I could tell when they were finished because the Holy Spirit alarms didn't go off anymore. It also proved to me that the witch was somewhere in their background and while they didn't operate in it, it was still impacting them. It also impacted how others perceived them.

They both had a rejection spirit attached to them prior to the repentance. That also went away as they did the repentance.

One of my students had a brother set to go to rehab for the third time after the Christmas holiday. This, again, was before I required my students to do the generational repentance. The Lord asked her to do the generational repentance after the semester ended but before Christmas. So, she worked hard at it and got it done. Her brother came to her in early January and said, "I don't know what happened but it's like the weight of the world came off my back and now I can get free of my own stuff." Wow. The weight of the generations did come off his back, and then he could deal with his stuff. He couldn't get free before because the generations were so heavy.

Generational repentance impacts all your relatives. When you do the repentance, everyone who has the same lineage as you gets set free. That means your parents, your siblings who have the same parents, and your aunts and uncles will get free because of you doing the generational repentance. Anyone who has another parent, like your children, will also have to do the repentance. My children got set free because both my husband and I did the generational repentance. They know that their future spouses will also have to do the generational repentance if it hasn't been done.

I've had people say they've done a lot of generational repentance and ask if they need to do Jacquelin Hanselman's book and Ron Horner's book? I tell them to humor me and do the work because I saw the three-foot-tall stack of documents in my vision and prior to that would have said that we'd already done a lot of repentance. One of the significant reasons God had Jacquelin Hanselman write her book was because it covered ancient sins. Most people haven't done those. And most people haven't done the judgments that Ron Horner's book covers.

I know that I want to move on and accomplish God's plan. That means we were to cover the generational repentance. My children and their children and their children don't have to because both my husband and I did the work.

TEARING DOWN THE HIGH PLACES

I was reading in the books of Kings in the Bible about the different kings and whether they had pleased the Lord with their service. One of the things He kept highlighting was whether they had taken down the "high places". For example, 1 Kings 12:30-31 says, "Now this thing became a sin, for the people went to worship before the one as far as Dan. He made shrines on the high places, and made priests from every class of people, who were not sons of Levi." And then it describes what King Josiah did in 2 Kings 23:8, "And he brought all the priests from the cities of Judah, and defiled the high places where the priests had burned incense, from Geba to Beersheba; also he broke down the high places at the gates which were at the entrance of the Gate of Joshua, the governor of the city, which were to the left of the city gate."

What are these "high places" and how do we please the Lord by tearing them down? In our personal lives it is generational repentance and deliverance. It is getting rid of all the sinful activities and thought processes that worshipped demonic gods and didn't serve the one true God. Once we do that, our families are free to serve the Lord and worship Him alone. It is still a choice, but we are free to make it once the family line is clear.

Corporately, I believe it will take identificational repentance, tearing down strongholds, and courts of heaven work to tear down the high places. At times, if you get enough people to do the generational repentance, the corporate breakthrough comes. We lived in Raleigh, NC for seven years and had so many people doing repentance from freemasonry that when one of the freemasonry lodge's properties in the city went up for sale because it no longer had enough members, I knew we had done a great work.

FREEMASONRY

Almost everyone on the planet has freemasonry somewhere in their background. Most of the freemasons are in the organization for business and networking contacts. They aren't aware of the evil and the worship of Lucifer at the highest levels. They are just normal humans who want to be successful in business and life. Unfortunately, by being in the organization, they and their families are subject to the curses. Getting out of the organization and repenting of having been in it is what tears down the high places and pleases God.

When I was thirty-one, I loved the Lord and had given Him my whole life. I had made a Lordship commitment nine months before that and got baptized in the Holy Spirit. The baptism opened my spiritual gifts as an adult and the demons tried to get me to sit back down in life. It was both glorious during my encounters with the Lord and at the same time a war with the enemy.

I had been going to a dermatologist for rosacea on my face and was taking tetracycline. My body also had been through both natural and spiritual hardships. I had just had three children in three and a half years and was facing some surgeries for repairing some of the injuries from pregnancy and childbirth. All those surgeries were scheduled for June. On Mother's Day weekend of that year, my back started really hurting in a place where I'd never felt pain before. By Saturday night, I was in a lot of pain and didn't feel well. By Sunday, I stayed home from church and stayed in bed and couldn't take care of my children. My husband stayed home and watched the children and took me to the doctor on Monday. The doctor knew it was liver related but didn't understand how bad it was. By Wednesday evening, I was in a hepatic coma in my room. We had been to the doctor multiple times and been to an outpatient clinic for tests. My limbs were twitching in big motions. My mom came to see me. She had been a hepatic nurse and knew the signs of liver failure. She also could be overly dramatic, so her diagnosis of liver failure was not believed when she told Joe.

Thursday night, my daughter's preschool teacher had a dream. In the dream God told her "Get up, call the head pastors, and pray because it's a battle for Annie's life unto the death." She took the dream literally, got up, called the head pastors of the two-thousand-member church we belonged to, and they all prayed for my life. The next morning, I got out of bed. I was healed but still had to walk out the impact of the liver failure. I got very jaundiced and itchy to the point where I took a dinner fork and dug deep into my hands and feet for relief from the major itching. I was miserable.

I also went to the Mayo Clinic for care and a diagnosis a few days later. My skin turned green, as well as the whites of my eyes, even my gums turned green. My doctor at Mayo Clinic was one of the most renowned in the world. He said it was liver failure; I was 6-12 hours from death, and he did not know how I survived it because the mortality rate for liver failure was 100%. He said if I had been at any emergency room I would have had a liver transplant had one been available.

The entire process took seven weeks and then another eighteen months to get my energy back. The biopsy I had at Mayo Clinic was inconclusive. The doctors assumed it was an allergy to tetracycline and told me to consider it lethal.

When I got home, we heard about the dream and prayer for my life to be saved. God had certainly intervened and saved my life. I asked God what had happened that caused the battle or if it was entirely physical. He told me I had freemasonry in my background and the liver failure was a result of that. I had never heard of freemasonry before the Lord mentioned it. I asked my parents about it; they hadn't heard of it. My grandfather was in the Elks club which is a subsidiary of freemasonry. I later got two prophetic words that I had freemasonry in my background.

Obviously, this was an extreme example. However, if you're going to operate in the courts of heaven, you need to be cleaned out generationally. I believe that almost everyone has freemasonry in their background somewhere, so it needs to be cleaned out.

Ask God here if there's any other generational repentance that you need to do.

_____
_____
_____
_____
_____
_____
_____
_____
_____
_____
_____
_____
_____
_____
_____
_____

MORE COURTS TIPS

There is no intercession in court work and we're not decreeing. It's a different kind of dispensation because we're partnering with God by coming to Him in His system. We always use our authority as believers, but in the courts, it looks like simply stating the case and knowing that God will then judge it. This system gives me so much faith in our Father. We're simply stating the case and knowing that He responds.

When I don't understand the situation, usually in metron cases and not personal cases, I will enter the courts, state the topic, and then pray in tongues. I know a case needs to be made, but sometimes I'm unaware of how to make it. I do this less than one percent of the time, but it's a helpful alternative when I don't know how to present a case.

I was rebuked by God once in court for yelling. I was emotional and upset and I yelled. That apparently is not the way to do a case. He rebuked me for yelling, told me He would always judge my cases, and if I understood the faith of getting my needs met, there was no need to yell.

God also told me no in a case once. He told me I didn't have the correct reasoning. I was exhausted, and I had asked Him if my husband and I could switch to a Solomon type season instead of a David season of battles. He told me we weren't Solomons. We were Davids, but we could switch from the battle season of David to the ruling and reigning of season of David.

In the courts, we always listen for any instruction God gives. I rarely get instructions now, but I did initially. In most of my cases I act as a feeler, meaning I can feel when something is done. I don't usually see anything or hear anything, but I always take the time to listen. God will speak or show us what's up if He wants to. I know that if He doesn't show me anything then the case is closed. He will instruct you at first as you're getting comfortable in court. That usually wanes as you become competent. So don't be uncomfortable or think anything is wrong if you're not hearing from God as you do courts cases.

The personal courts session is first. Then there are often more personal sessions. We did a lot of personal sessions when we had teenagers. There always seemed to be a lot going on. I listened to my children, and when I would hear them say something that didn't line up with the word of God, I'd explain the truth to them. If, after a couple of times they didn't get it, then I'd take it into the courts. Usually, within a week after the court case, I'd hear them speak truth. What happened in those cases was, the enemy was judged for lying to them. You're always asking God to judge the enemy and then people get free.

When our oldest daughter was a preteen, I had a dream. In the dream Beni Johnson told me our generational line looked good except our daughter had a Judas spirit. This was the spirit that sold Jesus to the enemy. This was before I knew about the courts. I prayed through it as well as I could and left it there. My daughter's teen years were rocky and full of rebellion. It was the courts that cut short the season, and ultimately the courts where God set her free.

There are certain areas we're each called to. I'm called to government, my husband is called to business, and my second daughter is called to family. So, despite my daughter being younger than my husband and I, my daughter has more authority for the family mountain. Our daughter was in ministry school and was away from our home. A few weeks before Christmas one year, I heard God say to ask my daughter if she would do a courts case for our family and our extended family. He added that she needed to fast for a few weeks before the case. I talked to her, and she'd already heard from God about fasting sugar for three weeks, was in the process, but didn't know why she was fasting.

I told her we'd come into court with her for support, but she'd be in charge of the case. After three weeks of fasting sugar, my daughter did a courts case for family and extended family. The results were extensive. Primarily, she asked God to remove the Judas spirit from our other daughter and that our family would pursue God. Our other daughter changed massively after that because she was finally freed. We also saw other family members begin to really walk with God in a way that they weren't able to before.

Ask God what other people's metrons are who you're in relationship with. You can know their strengths by knowing their metron.

_____
_____
_____
_____
_____
_____
_____
_____
_____
_____
_____
_____
_____
_____
_____
_____
_____
_____
_____
_____
_____
_____

IV.

TIMING, PROCESS, AND NAVIGATING HOPE DEFERRED

PERSONAL COURTS VS METRON COURTS

We all have things in our personal lives that need court work. When the bondage of generational sin is finished, the courts are then used to bring God's will into our metron. It's a very aggressive use of the courts for His will to be done. I have a friend who I had previously told about the courts. She did the generational repentance and then came to a class I was teaching in 2022. In the class, I took the class through the courts and then did a teaching on metrons. A metron is the area we are each called to where we have responsibility to govern like heaven governs. Her metron is the family mountain. She had experienced a lot of personal loss in her family yet had prophetic words from God saying what He would do. She held onto those words for years but didn't see any movement. Since her first court session it's been eighteen months, and one of her sons has not only completely turned his life around for the Father but is looking for a godly wife. She now has a different family. There's more work to be done but many blessings have come forth. She did the initial courts session for herself and then went into the courts many times for different things she saw. Fruit has come to the family. She feels like dreaming more with the Father, and the anxiety and depression have gone as her promises came to pass. She's a Hannah giving birth to a Samuel so there will be more personal breakthrough as the nation gets her breakthrough.

Our personal story with the Lord has looked like a lot of financial battles. Our prophetic words include being very wealthy. The Lord loves our lives walking with Him. One season was very long and full of lack and poverty. I had a dream where He showed me the poverty season was about sacrifice and that He cherished what we built with Him in relationship. If this is you, also, keep going! The Lord is so honored by your efforts and breakthrough will come. Even when it doesn't seem like the courts are effective, I can tell you they are. You are probably pushing on something that not only takes time but also will bring a great harvest of promises fulfilled.

I was talking to a former student about her process, where she did what the Lord had asked her to do for her future husband, someone she hadn't yet met. God asked her to do a courts session for her and for him. No fruit looked evident, but she continued to sow seeds. Then, she experienced a suddenly with God where she met her husband. He told her of what God had done in him over the previous few years, and she realized that her courts session really mattered for his process even though she hadn't seen the fruit in the natural yet. If you're not yet married and would like to be, ask God how you can partner with Him through the courts to prepare yourself and your husband for the coming match.

HOPE DEFERRED

In the fall of 2020, the Lord told me my heart was broken. I realized He was right. I had two major promises that hadn't happened yet, and I didn't see how they'd happen. It had been sixteen years since God had made those promises; It was a long and arduous time. He told me to read my friend's book, Seasons Change, by Emory Hornaday. While reading it, I saw that hope deferred was a season. One that would end. God spoke and said Proverbs 13:12 says, "Hope deferred makes the heart sick, but when the desire comes, it is a tree of life." He continued, "your heart is sick right now, but the promises will come and there will be life. And you can't write your other book for the making of a prophet until you've successfully navigated the hope deferred process. Two steps are left: the promise coming and the heart healing." I knew which two promises He was talking about and had hope they'd come. One of the promises came in the fall a year later, and the second one began a little over two years later.

If you have hope deferred or a broken heart, I want to encourage you to keep walking and the promises will come. Keep doing what you know to do because the Lord is faithful. Keep serving and keep doing courts cases. Your promises will open up even if it takes time for the nation to receive her promises.

Take a moment here and journal any promises you have that haven't yet come and where you are in the process. If you're in the hope deferred process, the promise coming and the heart healing are the final steps.

_____
_____
_____
_____
_____
_____
_____
_____
_____
_____
_____
_____
_____
_____

At the end of our lack season, my husband needed a better job. A prophet who we're in close relationship with would call me every three to four months and say, "The Rothschilds are sitting in your seat in the heavenlies. What are you going to do about it?" I'd ask the Lord and He would say not to do anything. I'd ask Joe just to be sure. He'd also hear not to touch it. Every three to four months for a couple of years, my prophet friend would ask me that question. In the fall of 2021, my friend called and asked the question again. While we were on the phone, I asked God if I could do anything about it. I heard Him say yes! I told my friend I'd call him back and as Joe came downstairs, I also asked him. He also heard yes. He heard to get my dad's gavel, clean it, and anoint it with oil, and do a court case.

I cleansed the gavel, anointed it with oil, and used it in my court case. It was very simple. I commanded all Rothschilds, all Rockefellers, and all unrighteous Kennedys to come out of their seats. I commanded the specific families God had chosen to get into the seats in the heavenlies. That is literally all I said. I banged down the gavel. If you remember the story from earlier, I had listened to the court case over the political and economic systems of the United States the day before and added my amen. That's why the court case was so easy and not convoluted.

While I was in court, I knew the American system of evil had just come down. I knew the world system still existed. I asked Him if I could take it down. He said no. Later, I called my friend back. He said he saw a huge boulder and about a quarter of it came off. He asked me if I could do the rest. I told him God had said no, at least for the time being.

Joe and I knew something powerful had happened. I asked God for confirmation in whatever way He wanted. The next day, as I came downstairs, I saw in the hallway to the bathroom what looked like a lump of grass or dirt on the floor. I didn't get close enough to see it and just made breakfast. When Joe came down, I told him about it and asked him to take care of it. He got close and looked at it. It was a dead toad! Why was there a dead toad in our house without us being aware of it? I knew it meant something prophetic but wasn't getting anything. I asked my friends to ask God about it. One of my friend's heard God say, "Tell Annie that great destruction came onto darkness yesterday." Confirmation of a successful court case.

A few days later, Joe and I did a court case for his dad's death. His dad had died six months before and there were still some items that hadn't been wrapped up. We did the court case and knew it was finished. Two days later, Joe got an email for a job interview for a director of operations position. A couple of weeks later, he started the job!

Do you see how both financial court cases were connected? One was a metron national case and the second was a personal extended family case. Once those two were finished, we were able to move into our personal breakthrough that was a further assignment.

I don't know if I will grow and will be able to take part of the world system or all of the world system down at some point. If you're reading this and don't live in the United States, or if you do, and have authority in areas of the world, ask Him if you can participate in bringing it down. I know He has a plan, and it may be your responsibility to partner with Him! God answers the question of "do I have authority and am I prepared to do this" very clearly. If you're not hearing a yes, it's not a yes.

I personally want to move as fast as the Lord will let me. He asked me when this journey with Him began after I made a Lordship commitment, if I wanted to go fast or slow. There's one speed for me and it's fast. He said, "Just so you know, when you go fast the crashes are bigger." The crashes are definitely bigger when you go fast. What took us eight years to accomplish in Redding, California would have taken us forty years if we'd gone slowly. Eight years was a whirlwind but forty would have been another generation's role to accomplish what we're beginning to walk in.

Take some time to talk to the Lord about your life, your journey, and your speed in getting there. There will be some of you who want to go slow and some who want to go fast. Whatever your speed, you need to know that the Lord is with you.

_____
_____
_____
_____
_____
_____
_____
_____
_____
_____
_____
_____
_____
_____
_____
_____
_____
_____
_____
_____
_____
_____
_____
_____

AUTHORITY AND YOUR METRON

Your metron of operating with God is the area you are called to in both the area and the scope or size of the area. As you grow, the area usually increases. My current metron is the political world and is the size of the United States now. I'm actually not sure when it encompassed the entire country, but it does now. You must ask God what the current size of your metron is so you stay in your lane of authority. I'm also called to Hollywood, but my sense is, it's not a current assignment and right now the area is small. It's also not on my heart to help Hollywood right now so that's another way to know what your assignment is.

Talk to God and ask Him about the journey you're on regarding your metron. Ask Him if and how it will grow and anything else you need to know so that you're not wandering in the wilderness.

_____
_____
_____
_____
_____
_____
_____
_____
_____
_____
_____
_____
_____
_____
_____
_____
_____

I've done all kinds of metron cases in the political world with God. This is the type of case that makes a big difference in the world. The cases are usually easy and relevant to the present. I usually hear from God about them by either being passionate about them or not having thought about them at all. All of a sudden, it'll occur to me to do a case in the matter. However you hear from

God, metron cases come from relationship with God. It's a partnership and not a formula, meaning, I could come up with all kinds of cases to do on my own, yet God knows the timing and which ones to do. Even saying that, I also have a responsibility regarding doing cases. It's a balance between God telling me to do cases and me taking responsibility. Doing cases is like doing a dance with God. He doesn't want us to be puppets where we only do what He says or says not to do. And He definitely doesn't want us to be out of relationship where He says to us, "Many will say to Me in that day, 'Lord, Lord, have we not prophesied in Your name, cast out demons in Your name, and done many wonders in Your name?' And then I will declare to them, 'I never knew you; depart from Me, you who practice lawlessness'" as in Matthew 7:22-23.

THE BALANCE AND RESPONSIBILITY OF WALKING WITH GOD

It's the balance of walking in the fear of the Lord and the love of the Lord. If you walk in the middle of both of those you won't get into sloppy grace or the understanding of the Father not being good. He is absolutely good and absolutely the judge. We are so loved. And so His children. And so beholden to Him.

When we know who we are in God, and know whose we are, we can bring health and safety to this earth. We do this through the courts cases we do. We do it by not allowing the darkness to reign. People can get to know Christ and live for Him.

There's a Scripture in Psalms 84 that talks about timing. Verse 10 says, "For a day in your courts is better than a thousand elsewhere. I would rather be a doorkeeper in the house of my God than dwell in the tents of the wicked" NIV Here the psalmist is talking about serving in the house of God within the inner court and the outer court. However, this language about the courts is literal in our time. It means to do court work. The timing of court work is either immediate breakthroughs or processes starting when we do the court work. You can take that to the bank. Breakthroughs literally come immediately rather than taking one thousand days or years to come to pass as with prayer.

Even so, not everything is instant. Some things take time. I'm not sure if it's just a natural process, or if there's warfare along the way. My husband's PPO loan for his company went through during Covid but his unemployment for himself didn't. That took some court work to accomplish and took four months to come through.

The Lord uses the courts to build faith in our lives. My son had some warts on his hands, and he wanted to go to the doctor to treat them. Our finances were tight, so I thought we could try the anti-fungal treatment ourselves. In the meantime, one of his friends in another state also had warts on his hands and went to the doctor. He was left with several scars from the treatment. At that point, my son didn't believe the anti-fungal home treatment would work and didn't want scars from the doctor's treatment, so he asked me if we could go into court for treatment instead. We went into court for the warts. God healed them right away with no scars. This was a faith building exercise about the courts for my son.

There are some things that we don't know why they're happening. So, we combine asking God what the problem is with going into the courts. For example, I had an acne problem on my chin. My skin is normally clear and healthy looking. I couldn't get the acne to clear up with skin care treatment. Finally, I asked God what was going on. He told me I was drooling during the night and to take it into the courts. So, I did. The acne instantly cleared up. Whether the acne was a natural occurrence or a demonic occurrence, I don't know. But I know the God who has the answers!

When I say I "see" things, I "see" them on the screen of my imagination. All my court work to this point has been with that "seer" system. The other parts of "seeing" include open visions where you "see" things with your eyes wide open like watching a movie. I have seen open visions before, but I have not seen them like that in court. If you do, great. If you don't, great. It doesn't matter how you see or if you just go by faith. God is okay with either. I want you to be okay and know that you can operate in the courts of heaven how you are and how you interact with God. The important thing is that we're doing the work to change the earth. However, pornography and sexual sin cloud and convolute the seer screen. If that's on your screen, you need to repent and not do that anymore. It really matters to God that we are clean and represent Jesus on this earth.

About five years ago, my brother ended up in the ICU with a double lung infection. It progressed over a couple of weeks to a few heart attacks because of the strain on his lungs and heart. He was in a coma and was dying in the hospital. My husband and I did a court case at that time. As we were in court, the Lord told me that my brother didn't want to live. I told Joe what the Lord had said. Joe had already heard the Lord say that to him, too. I cried about the sadness of that truth. After I finished crying, we did some court work on behalf of my family line regarding my dad and his wanting to also give up in life. Once we had that finished, we spoke to my brother's spirit and told him it was his choice, but we'd like him to live. The next thing Joe and I both saw, but told each other about it after we saw it, was an angel opening a door to the courtroom. It was a door to the spare parts room in heaven. The angel brought in two new lungs and a new heart. We were both handed these items. I stood there not sure what to do with them, so I asked God. God said to take them down the hall to the surgical room in heaven. We took them there and saw my brother lying in a bed with doctors working on him. An angel took the lungs and heart and walked to my brother's bed. That was the last we saw in heaven. About five minutes later, I got a text from my sister saying my brother had awakened from his coma. He was healed and out of the hospital shortly after that.

Our court work gave my brother time to put things right with his son and with God. However, he still chose to exit earth early. About four years later my brother died of liver failure from alcohol abuse. God always gives us a choice and always cheers us on for life. It's up to each one of us what we do with it.

OFFENSE

We can use the courts not only to do defense but also to do offense in our lives. As we get going, we will use the courts more for offense and for the discipling of nations. We have many things to do for God in this world, and it'll take the courts to do it.

I self-published my first three books. For my fourth book, Reaganista, God told me to get a publisher, and He'd help me. He also told me to sow a financial seed for a publisher. So, I sowed the seed and did a courts case. Then I researched for a week and got all my paperwork in place to send out. I found nine publishers and two agents who would be possibilities for my work and sent my query letters out. A couple of weeks later, one of the publisher's responded to me and wanted to publish my book! It was truly a quick answer to asking God for help in the courts. We can always trust God to be faithful.

At this point, I don't give the enemy time to set up a plan against me or my work. I don't let a tug of war happen. Before I had the revelation of the courts, it seemed like I was constantly battling the enemy for any forward movement. Life is much easier this way--and more fun with God. This way I can do many more court cases for the nation.

When my husband got his new job, the company paid for a furnished apartment for us for six months. Towards the end of the time in the apartment, I wanted to live in a house. I have a hard time living in an apartment because of how close the people are to us. I asked God for a new house, granite countertops, nice floors, and a garage. I did a court case making my request. Then I quickly found two new houses for rent. We went and looked at both and I picked the one I wanted. It was brand new with granite countertops. It was a one-story house in a very nice neighborhood with an acre of land. It was actually less expensive than the apartment and the company agreed to rent it for us for another year as we settled into our new community.

WHEN CHANGE IS NOT IMMEDIATE

There are some court cases that take a process or don't seem to work. We seemed to have bed bugs in our bedroom for four months. My husband and I were both getting bit on our extremities as we slept. We were gone for five weeks on different trips and were fine when we were away. My husband had checked and never found any bed bugs or signs of them anywhere, but we treated the bed and the room and continued to get bit. I even went to the dermatologist regarding it. We had done court cases for it and the courts didn't seem to help. The entire process was traumatizing. Finally, I scheduled a bug exterminator to come. He came and looked through the room, the mattresses, and everywhere and told us we didn't have bed bugs. He didn't know what to tell us but that the bed bugs didn't exist. That somehow broke the battle, and it stopped. Despite the literal scars on our arms, legs, and feet, the battle was over. I asked God about it later and heard Him say, "It was a traumatic demonic spirit." Meaning it could have encompassed anything, but the main function was trauma.

Our financial process was a process that took seventeen years. It only ended once I did the courts case on the Rothschilds, Rockefellers, and Kennedys. Despite using the courts for six years, it was the final court case that changed our situation into prosperity. And it changed instantly as soon as I did that case.

There are lots of reasons that courts don't change things immediately in your personal life. It can be because of wilderness seasons or if you're pushing on a national issue like Hannah in Scripture. It can be the timing of God or if you have active sin or unforgiveness. Other reasons include if you're free will isn't lining up with what God is doing, if your soul is unhealthy or addicted and healing is needed, or if you're untangling a web and God needs to continue unlocking keys. All I know is, if you keep walking with God in earnest, He will set you free and help you bring keys to the things He's appointed you to do.

CLUES TO FOLLOWING GOD IN COURT

If you're not sure what to do in the courts, there are tools to help you. For example, whatever is in your personal or family line can give you clues for how to help people. What you've overcome you can help others with. Things that stir your heart can help you set other people free. What makes you angry? That can be a clue for how to move people forward. What problems do you want to solve? You're unique. The things that you're interested in are unique and the world needs your input! What's in your metron and your mountain? Those areas have lots of things the Lord wants you to partner with Him in.

As you grow in favor and authority, your ability to do court work increases.

PRAYER VS OPERATING IN THE COURTS

What's the difference between prayer and the courts of heaven? The Courts bring justice. It's God's way of ruling. Prayer is still needed for various things. When my grandson needed surgery as a baby, I took the case through the court and then asked friends to join me in prayer for the different issues. For example, surgery was scheduled for 11:30 am and my grandson wasn't allowed to eat past 4 am. That's a long time for a six-month-old not to eat and to not understand why. His mother got him up at 4 am for a bottle and then

God did the rest because he was happy and smiling all morning while he waited to be taken back for surgery. I could feel the grace of God on the entire situation because of the prayer coverage.

I can usually feel prayer coverage. One day, I didn't feel like writing this book or any other book for the rest of my life—haha! I knew the enemy was creating some havoc. I can always tell when I have enough prayer coverage because writing with prayer coverage is like driving a speed boat across the lake with the wind blowing my hair back. It goes well, is enjoyable, and doesn't take a lot of time. When I don't have enough prayer coverage, it feels like I'm swimming and pulling the speed boat behind me! It's not a fun experience for sure. Our lives should have a grace to it, and God provides that grace through prayer coverage. It's one way that we need other people. We were not meant to do life alone, so prayer is important. Please don't stop praying. But please add the courts to your toolbox.

Now that you've read this book on the courts of heaven, you're ready to begin your journey. My prayer for you is that you're successful and that you enjoy your time with God. Ask God if there's anything else you specifically need to know. Journal it here.

_____
_____
_____
_____
_____
_____
_____
_____
_____
_____
_____
_____
_____

Thank you for your time and helping bring heaven to earth!

Opening Prayer- (A)

Father, I thank You for _____. Please bless him/her and his/her entire family line. Bless this person and their entire family line and me and my entire family in all areas: physically, spiritually, and emotionally. Protect all our computers, Wi-Fi, spaces, finances, health, relationships and everything that concerns us, in Your name.

Mercy Court - (B)

The mercy court requires repentance or confession of sin. In this court, I use this sheet and the Mercy Court Master Sheet of sins to confess. It is the blood of Jesus that washes us clean and allows us to reconcile with the Father. After we are finished confessing sin, we ask God for mercy for us, that we wouldn't have the consequences of sin but would receive God's mercy instead.

<u>Mercy Court</u>

Thank you, God for coming into Your mercy court.

I forgive _____ for any sin against me and I release him/her from my judgments. I bless him/her and ask You to bless him/her. (Ask Holy Spirit for anyone to forgive. Move to the next step if you don't hear of anyone else.)

Father, I confess the following as sin: _____. (Confess any and all sins on the Courts Master Sheet and on your personal sheet of family problems.)

(Take a moment here and "look" into the cloud of witnesses to see who is giving heavenly testimony on your behalf. Usually, members of your family who have gone to heaven will show up for your court case.)

Father, I ask for Your mercy for repenting of sins and for Your forgiveness. (Ask God if there's anything else you need to confess here. If so, confess it and ask for mercy.)

Father, I ask You for justice and restoration. Specifically, _____ (anything you need returned or restored.)

Thank you, Father, for the mercy court. Amen.

Courts Master Sheet by Annie Blouin - (C)

Revised 4/27/22
Special thanks to Robert Henderson, Jacqueline and Dan Hanselman, and Ron Horner for all of their pioneering revelatory work in the Courts of Heaven, bringing leadership, strategy, freedom, and strength to the Body of Christ.

Mercy Court- Master Sheet (requires repentance)

*Sexual sin- pornography, lust, premarital sex/activity, homosexuality, bestiality, adultery, assault, pedophilia, incest, gender identity confusion, prostitution, licentiousness
*Rebellion to Authority (natural and spiritual)- parental, sexual, dishonoring government, dishonor of leadership.
*Covenant breaking- divorce, adultery, betrayal, unequally yoked, ungodly alliances in marriage.
*Disobedience to God's voice-
*Innocent Bloodshed- murder, abortion, unauthorized acts of war
*Abuse of Authority-
*Rewards evil for good- abusing others to climb corporate ladder
*(The 7 above categories apply to all family lines somewhere in the generational blood- line per Robert Henderson.)

Addiction- alcoholism, drug abuse, gambling, gluttony, sugar, workaholic, food, shopping, anger, smoking, sleep as an escape, sleeping pills, prescription drugs

Financial- not tithing, not offering, not taking care of poor, not stewarding money well, theft, shoplifting, greed, entitlement, poverty

Fear- worry, obsession, unbelief, hesitation/not walking through doors God opens, dread, impatience, defeatism

Control- partnering with Jezebel, suicide, impatience, greed, bullying, analyzing/assuming what others are thinking, word curses, independence/lone ranger, led by feelings, lying, self-sufficiency, self-righteousness, witchcraft, not submitting to God's Lordship, building own kingdom, using God's favor for own political gain, rebellion, bribery, meanness, defiance, using God and people, domination, emasculation, inverted relationships, overreaching, religion, perfectionism, legalism, lack of trusting God, determinism, powerlessness

Rejection- self-hatred, insecurity, victimhood, suicide, self-sabotage, dishonor of own talents

Pride- partnering with Leviathan, false humility, selfishness, judging others, easily offended, jealousy, not helping others to rise, false pretenses, intellectualism, superiority, snobbery, false humility, covetousness, needs to be right, condemnation, falsely accusing or using God, self-centeredness, unwillingness to forgive,

Abuse- anger, verbal, physical, emotional abandonment, betrayal, rage, misogyny, racism, slave ownership, subservient women, cursing own children, domestic violence

Lack of discipline- not taking care of self-spirit/soul/body, irresponsibility, laziness, not stewarding time/finances/gifts//favor well, wanting only to "chill", lack of motivation, dirty house or car, not being spiritual leader in home

Broken promises- usury

Illegal access to seer realm- occult, drug use, hookah, pornography

Occult- horoscopes, Ouija boards, tarot cards, satanic rituals, fortune telling, freemasonry, yoga, numerology, seer gift not connected to Holy Spirit, Druidism, Egyptology

False Religions- Mormonism, Islam, Buddhism, New Age, religious spirit, Jehovah Witness, not worshipping Jesus in Spirit and Truth, religious form instead of relationship, legalism, worshipping nature

Appellate Court - (D)

The appellate court means "appeals". You are asking God for anything that has not gone in your favor to be appealed. That's the "negative" side of things. And here, we also submit our prophetic words, promises from God and promises from Scripture to happen on our behalf. This is the "positive" side of things. The mercy court only deals with "negative" things (sin). The appellate court can deal with either "negative" or "positive" things.

Appellate Court

Father, I come into your appellate court.

Thank you for the negative things that are being appealed and the positive things that are happening. Specifically, _____. (Use the appellate court master sheet here and add anything from your personal sheet.)

Father, I specifically ask for restitution in _____. (This is where you ask for money returned, relationships restored, jobs, people saved, etc.)

Father, I submit my prophetic words/promises here. _____.

Thank You. Amen.

Appellate Court- Master Sheet - (E)

To bring an appeal (false judgments being repealed. Or asking God to bring about promises of God/prophetic words not yet fulfilled)

(can present it either in negative or positive form for the Appellate Court)

Body Health- asthma, diabetes, heart disease, stroke, blood clots, varicose veins, cancer, Alzheimer's, scoliosis, headaches, migraines, early death, liver disease, hepatitis, organ failure, cold sores, HIV/AIDS, obesity/overweight, high blood pressure, high cholesterol, fatigue, acne, allergies, sleep apnea, snoring, poor sleep, memory, healing for injuries, arthritis, bad hips/knees/joints, thyroid/adrenals, body pain, healthy bladder control, dyslexia/learning disabilities, any other physical illness, blood circulation, ulcer colitis, hormonal balance, healthy body Image, skin eczema, lactose intolerance, gluten intolerance, vaccine injuries, calcified heart, infertility, epilepsy, miscarriages/stillbirths, auto immune diseases,

Spirit/Soul Health- depression, anxiety, night terrors, fear, bi-polar, schizophrenia, suicide, autism/Asperger's, ADD/ADHD, focus, confusion, torment, panic attacks, children as a burden, dyslexia, agitation

Prophetic words/Promises from God
Financial loss or cap on finances, financial independence, financial breakthrough
Any injustices
Seer gift/prophetic gift/ability to hear God
Communicate well with others/be understood
Identify and connect to own emotions
Business anointing
Deep sadness/family brokenness
Relationship restoration
Family/friends salvation
Concussions/head trauma/learning disabilities
Car accidents/windshield chips/freak accidents
Love well
Connection to Holy Spirit
Body odor/bad breath/drooling

Allergies to poison ivy/oak/sumac
Weird physical ailments
Belief/Trust/Humility
Freedom from sin/shame cycle
Freedom from addiction and addictive behavior
Domestic violence
Divine order in family/relationships/children/work/marriage/children
Own a home
Employment
Love and fear the Lord
Purity
Acceptance
Ability to rest
Redeemed Manhood/Womanhood
Motivation/Patience/Not be lonely
Self-love
Free from offense/fear/bitterness/self-hatred/pride/control/rejection
Healthy menstrual cycles for women
Freedom from cults/proselytizing
Know times/seasons
Healthy time management
Family unity
Child custody/support/alimony
Word curses broken
Weird family curses/destructive patterns (ex. People die at 40 from strokes)
Healthy discernment
Fear of man
Favor with God and man
Being celebrated
Voice being heard
Ability to create wealth
Justice
Strong, healthy spirit
Healthy confrontation, boundaries, awareness of other's feelings

Healthy communication
Sound mind
Mental health
Sleep as rest
Holy Spirit as comforter
Divine destiny
Visibility and Honor
In sync with timing and order
Delays
False understandings/Misunderstandings/Misinterpretations
Opposition to land
Reputation
Contacts and Connections ordained by God
Money
Marital Unity
Family Destiny
Infertility- spiritually and naturally
Details
Cleaning as associated to the role of a woman
False perceptions
Mental limitations
Generational mantles, blessings, and inheritances
Skewed perceptions of wealth
Taskmaster, Slavedriver

Trophy Room Protocol - (F)

Trophy Room in Hell Protocol

It is our right to go with Jesus to the trophy room in hell to get back what was stolen from us and our generational line after we've repented of sin in Heaven's mercy court. Unless Jesus directs you personally, at a later time, there's only a need to go into the trophy room once. Common things found in the trophy room are finances, relationships, spouses, children, destiny, etc.

Steps:
1. Repent of your own sin and generational sin in mercy court
2. Freeze and silence trophy room in Jesus' name so that we go in unhindered
3. Use the Master Sheet/Trophy Room guide to declare items you are taking back
4. Hand all items to Jesus. He will give you back each item as you are ready to steward it
5. Ask Jesus if there's anything else in there you've missed. Declare, pick up, and hand to Jesus
6. Tell Jesus thank you!
7. Unfreeze and un-silence the trophy room

Trophy Room- Master Sheet - (G)

Divine Health
Finances
Love (for self, God, others)
Energy
Focus/Passion/Motivation
Healthy Marriage
Healthy Family Relationships
Self-respect
Belief
Healthy Communication
Peace/Joy
Purity
Responsibility
Leadership
Justice
Financial Prosperity (tithing and offering, $, house, car, debts paid off, investments, income, retirement, inheritance)
Enjoy work
Submission to God and authority
Self-control
Hearing God's voice
Legacy
Honor mother and father
Business anointing
Creativity
Writing
Seer/prophetic gift
Evangelism
Acceptance
Rest
Sweet Sleep
God Dreams
Clear skin
Patience
Fruit of the Spirit
Friends salvation
Relationship restoration

Safety/Protection
Courage/boldness
Favor
Fear of the Lord
Healthy moral grid
Healthy thyroid/bladder/kidneys/organs
Pain free body/soul
Belief
Deep relationship with God
Open doors
Healthy friendships
Prophetic promises
Time Management
Spiritual gifts
Artistic/creative gifts
Voice
Business contracts
Mind of Christ
Wisdom/Revelation
Children
Family salvation
Adventures
Team
Toys
Vacations
Healing gift
Color Vision
Clear Vision
Longevity
Plan/Strategies
Graced Dying Process for family/self
Healthy Spine
Healthy veins/valves/blood flow
Healthy Business Partners
Healing from Trauma
Great Memory

Fun
Order
Hormonal balance
Focus, clarity of mind
In sync with timing and order
Visibility
Honor
Freedom
Sound Mind
Healthy confrontation, boundaries, awareness of other's feelings, communication
Sleep as rest
Holy Spirit as comforter
Celebrated by people
Mental health
Protection
Protection and Recovery from disaster
Accurate perspective
Happiness
Honesty
Divine Alignment
Ability to be still
Celebrations
Full recovery
Dreams
Fun
Community
Stewardship
Ability to hold onto things
Inheritance/Gold/Money/Oil Energy
Restored Reputation
Recognition
Unity
Teamwork
Power

Promotion
Wisdom
Wonder
Blessing
Capacity
Wholeness
Quality of life
Harvests from generosity
Identity
Income Streams
Authority
Contentment
Multiplication
Family
Jobs
Healthy pancreas
Business Acumen
Business Opportunity
Advancement
Debt free/Freedom from debt
Expansion
Fitness
Honor
Laughter
Holiness
Fear of the Lord

*Be sure to write in any additional items for Mercy Court/Appellate Court/Trophy Room that apply to you and your family.

Court of Times and Seasons - (H)

This is the court where we adjust the time to coincide with the timing of God after doing the other court work. It usually speeds up the family time to achieve what God has for the family. You will "see" or "know" that the angels are adjusting the clocks for the family. I usually see a grandfather clock adjust to 12. The grandfather clock is the clock for the entire family.

Father, thank you for Your court of times and seasons. I ask that Your angels adjust all the family clocks for my entire generational line to align with Your timing.

(Watch and see what you see.)

Amen.

Sealing Prayer - (I)

Father, I seal all the work done here, in the courts and in the family line and I ask that You bless this family. Please bring all their prophetic words and promises to pass. I pray protection over their entire family and my entire family in all areas of finances, health, jobs, relationships, and everything that is owned and stewarded. Thank You for protecting us all in Your mighty name.

Courts of Heaven Scriptures

• Psalms 82:1-6 TPT

1 All rise! For God now comes to judge as he convenes heaven's courtroom. He judges every judge and rules in the midst of the gods, saying,

2 "How long will you judges refuse to listen to the voice of true justice and continue to corrupt what is right by judging in favor of the wrong?"

Pause in his presence

3 "Defend the defenseless, the fatherless and the forgotten, the disenfranchised and the destitute.

4 Your duty is to deliver the poor and the powerless; liberate them from the grasp of the wicked.

5 But you continue in your darkness and ignorance while the foundations of society are shaken to the core!

6 Didn't I commission you as judges, saying, 'You are all like gods, since you judge on my behalf. You are all like sons of the Most High, my representatives.'

• Daniel 7:9-10 NKJV

9 "I watched till thrones were put in place, and the Ancient of Days was seated; His garment was white as snow, and the hair of His head was like pure wool. His throne was a fiery flame, its wheels a burning fire;

10 A fiery stream issued and came forth from before Him. A thousand thousands ministered to Him; ten thousand times ten thousand stood before Him. The court was seated, and the books were opened.

- Daniel 7:26-27 NKJV

26 'But the court shall be seated, and they shall take away his dominion, to consume and destroy it forever.

27 Then the kingdom and dominion, and the greatness of the kingdoms under the whole heaven, shall be given to the people, the saints of the Most High. His kingdom is an everlasting kingdom, and all dominions shall serve and obey Him.'

- Matthew 5:25-26 AMP

25 Come to terms quickly [at the earliest opportunity] with your opponent at law while you are with him on the way [to court], so that your opponent does not hand you over to the judge, and the judge to the guard, and you are thrown into prison.

26 I assure you and most solemnly say to you, you will not come out of there until you have paid the last cent.

- Matthew 5:25-26 NKJV

25 Agree with your adversary quickly, while you are on the way with him, lest your adversary deliver you to the judge, the judge hand you over to the officer, and you be thrown into prison.

26 Assuredly, I say to you, you will by no means get out of there till you have paid the last penny.

- Matthew 25-26 TPT

25 It is always better to come to terms with the one who wants to sue you before you go to trial, or you may be found guilty by the judge, and he will hand you over to the officers, who will throw you into prison.

26 Believe me, you won't get out of prison until you have paid the full amount!"

- Isaiah 43:25-26 NKJV

25 "I, even I, am He who blots out your transgressions for My own sake; and I will not remember your sins.

26 Put Me in remembrance; let us contend together; state your case, that you may be acquitted.

- Isaiah 43:25-26 AMP

25 "I, only I, am He who wipes out your transgressions for My own sake, and I will not remember your sins.

26 Remind Me [of your merits with a thorough report], let us plead and argue our case together; state your position, that you may be proved right.

- Psalms 84:1-2, 10 NKJV

1 How lovely is Your tabernacle, O Lord of hosts!

2 My soul longs, yes, even faints for the courts of the Lord; my heart and my flesh cry out for the living God.

10 For a day in Your courts is better than a thousand. I would rather be a doorkeeper in the house of my God than dwell in the tents of wickedness.

- 2 Kings 18:1-7 NKJV

1 Now it came to pass in the third year of Hoshea the son of Elah, king of Israel, that Hezekiah the son of Ahaz, king of Judah, began to reign.

2 He was twenty-five years old when he became king, and he reigned twenty-nine years in Jerusalem. His mother's name was Abi the daughter of Zechariah.

3 And he did what was right in the sight of the Lord, according to all that his father David had done.

4 He removed the high places and broke the sacred pillars, cut down the wooden image and broke in pieces the bronze serpent that Moses had made; for until those days the children of Israel burned incense to it, and called it Nehushtan.

5 He trusted in the Lord God of Israel, so that after him was none like him among all the kings of Judah, nor who were before him.

6 For he held fast to the Lord; he did not depart from following Him, but kept His commandments, which the Lord had commanded Moses.

7 The Lord was with him; he prospered wherever he went. And he rebelled against the king of Assyria and did not serve him.

- Psalm 24 NKJV

1 The earth is the Lord's, and all its fullness, the world and those who dwell therein.

2 For He has founded it upon the seas, and established it upon the waters.

3 Who may ascend into the hill of the Lord? Or who may stand in His holy place?

4 He who has clean hands and a pure heart, who has not lifted up his soul to an idol, nor sworn deceitfully.

5 He shall receive blessing from the Lord, and righteousness from the God of his salvation.

6 This is Jacob, the generation of those who seek Him, who seek Your face. Selah

7 Lift up your heads, O you gates! And be lifted up, you everlasting doors! And the King of glory shall come in.

8 Who is this King of glory? The Lord strong and mighty, the Lord mighty in battle.

9 Lift up your heads, O you gates! Lift up, you everlasting doors!
And the King of glory shall come in.

10 Who is this King of glory? The Lord of hosts, He is the King of glory. Selah

RECOMMENDED RESOURCES

Silencing the Accuser: Restoration of Your Birthright, Third Edition by Jacquelin and Dan Hanselman. (Best found on lulu.com)

Jubileeresources for freemasonry repentance prayer.
https://shop.jubileeresources.org/en-us/pages/freemasonry?_pos=1&_sid=1fc7fea7b&_ss=r

Overturning the False Verdicts of Freemasonry by Ron L Horner. (Best found on lulu.com)

Druid repentance prayer. https://www.kanaanministries.org/wp-content/uploads/2019/02/Druidism-Prayer-1.pdf

kanaanministries.org Any other generational repentance prayers that are highlighted to you.

The Killing of Uncle Sam: The Demise of the United States of America by Rodney Howard-Browne and Paul L. Williams

The Killing of the Planet: How a Financial Cartel Doomed Mankind by Rodney Howard-Browne and Paul L. Williams

Victorious Eschatology: A Partial Preterist View by Dr. Harold R. Eberle and Martin Trench

Seasons Change: A Poetry Collection by Emory Colvin

The Seven Mountain Renaissance: Vision and Strategy through 2050 by Johnny Enlow

Also, by Annie Blouin

Everlasting Prophetic

Bridging Heaven to Earth

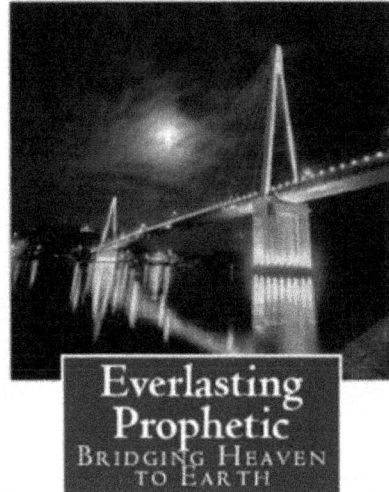

Prophetic Revelation

Keys to Spiritual Maturity

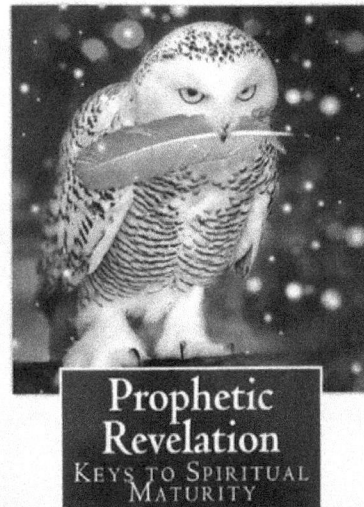

Everlasting Doors

When the Supernatural Penetrates American Politics

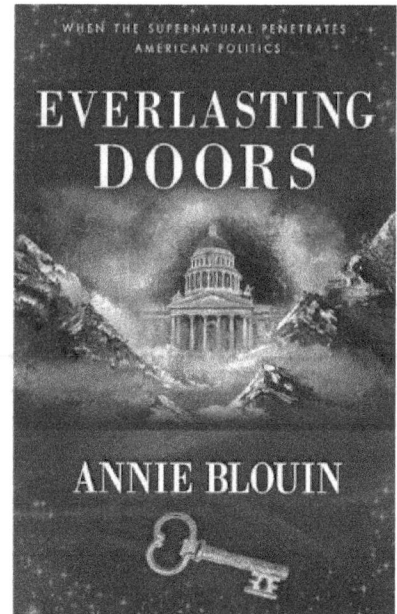

Reaganista

Heaven's Blueprints for America's Return to Glory

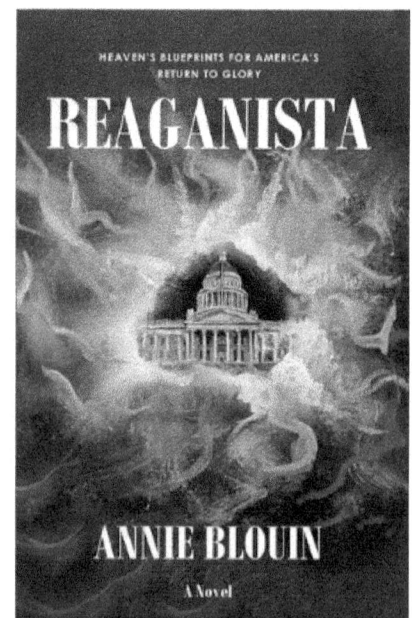

www.ingramcontent.com/pod-product-compliance
Lightning Source LLC
Chambersburg PA
CBHW052341100426

42736CB00046B/3338